IF I KNE

THEN WHAT I
KNOW NOW

Life Skills Strategies for Success
From Today's Student-Athlete Leaders

Foreword by Dr. Cedric Dempsey
Former NCAA President and Executive Director
1994-2002

Read Quotes From Student-Athletes On:

- Time management

- Study Skills

- The importance of good nutrition

- Leadership

- Transferable Skills

- Goal setting

- Creating a balanced experience

- Managing your money

- Life in the dorms

- Dealing with injuries

- Doing well your freshman year

- Handling stress

- Communication skills

- *MUCH MORE!!*

Praise for:
If I Knew Then What I Know Now

"We are all looking for bits of inspiration and insights. This book is loaded with great tips - practical, helpful, everyday things, that if done, can make a huge difference! It's as motivational as it is educational. Although geared toward student-athletes, it's really a book about succeeding in life. A great read for parents, coaches and teachers too!" **Lute Olson, Hall of Fame Basketball Coach, University of Arizona**

"Success in life is about more than being good in your sport. And what separates great players sometimes has nothing to do with the game itself. This book shows you why developing in all areas can be the most important thing you ever do. It lays the groundwork for what it takes to be a winner – in your sport and in life." **Doug Weight, St. Louis Blues, 3-Time All Star, 2-Time Olympian**

"This book has an uplifting and inspirational tone that made me enjoy reading it and want to read on. It addresses pertinent issues that can be applied to student-athletes at any college or university. I enjoyed the quotations from famous people in history and especially those by the student- athletes. What they say is valid, insightful and makes a lot of sense. I enjoyed being able to read through the quotations and identify with one of the sports, but at the same time I found it important to be able to see the diverse responses of those athletes in different sports. I like the rhetorical questions throughout the book. It helped me as a reader engage and really think about what I was reading. As an athlete, I found the application of many of the concepts to athletics to be especially helpful." **Kelly McCabe, Former Softball Player University of Virginia**

"This book will be instrumental in helping student-athletes stay balanced, not be overwhelmed and achieve their goal of attaining a college degree. Excellent!" **Bob Elliott, University of Arizona Basketball and Track Letterman; Verizon/GTE Academic All America Hall of Fame**

"We will be using it for sure next fall for our class. It is great and follows closely what we are presently doing...without a book. I haven't previously found one that I thought fit our needs. We will look forward to putting it to use!" **Karen Nelson, Assistant Athletics Director, University of Oregon**

"If I Knew Then What I Know Now is a dynamic, fully integrated approach to the real life problems of student-athletes. Helping student-athletes acquire life skills that both enhance and drive personal effectiveness is the core of this books promise---and that promise is delivered in a genuinely exciting way. Superb!" **Dr. Jim Loehr, Sport Psychologist, CEO, LGE Performance Systems**

"Over the years, I have strongly encouraged my teams to get involved with our Life Skills program (C.A.T.S.). Without question, it has helped them create BALANCE in their life, become more well-rounded and have a better overall college experience. This book can help tremendously in getting freshmen off to a strong start that will positively affect everything that they do. If you want to be successful in your sport and in life, read this book!" **Mike Candrea, Softball Coach University of Arizona, 6 National Championships, USA Olympic Head Coach 2004**

"This book will be a welcome addition to BBH 048 (Our Life Skills class). I like that it allows students to assess where they are in each of the five areas of CHAMPS/Life Skills, while also giving them an opportunity to learn from student-athletes across the country. I endorse the book enthusiastically!" **Sue Sherburne, Faculty member-Biobehavioral Health, Program Administrator, Nagle CHAMPS/Life Skills Program, Penn St. University**

"The CHAMPS Program definitely helped shape my college experience. This book will be a great help to any incoming student and student-athletes will be able to relate to it because of all the shared experiences. Information like this can also simplify the transition into college. It will be nice for student-athletes to have a reliable resource based on what they really need to know. I sure wish I would have had it when I was a freshman - it would have saved me a lot of headaches!" **Andrea Neary-Dutoit, NCAA Woman of the Year Finalist; NCAA Champion, Pole Vault**

"How wonderful and lucky to have a book that offers such insight, guidance and information! Not only for the student-athlete, but for parents, teachers and coaches too. This is a book about life, not just athletics. Where was something like this when I was about to embark on my next journey through college? I will be using it in numerous ways now though – it's great!" **Ann Meyers Drysdale, Olympian, Naismith Basketball Hall of Fame, 3-Sport Athlete at UCLA, Broadcaster, and Mother of 3 with the late Baseball Hall of Famer, Don Drysdale.**

"This book naturally inspires you to apply the same focus and persistence you have in your sport to the rest of your life. It puts a fun and personal approach to your academic and life goals and reminds you that you're not alone on your journey!" **Kimberly Cobb, Faculty, Freshman Seminar Course: College Focus, Colorado Mountain College**

"I know how much athletic competition contributed to my own personal development. I believe that the life skills strategies presented in this book will be very helpful to student-athletes today, who live in more complex environments than I experienced, and may need more explicit direction in their development." **Dr. Peter Likins, President, University of Arizona, Former Student-Athlete at Stanford University**

"I learned so much in college and because of all my experiences I now feel prepared for the next phase of my life. This book covers just about everything you can go through. It's comforting to know lots of us went through the same things. I couldn't stop reading the quotes – they're so true!" **Jennie Finch, USA Softball, Honda Award winner, College World Series MVP 2001**

"I love this book. It makes you think, yet provides an easy to follow approach that you can put to immediate use. It identifies key areas to analyze and the quotes reinforce those ideas. I found P-Factor Analysis to be a great evaluation tool. It's different from any other book I have read. Complete, concise and thoroughly enjoyable!" **Mary Bowman, Assistant Athletics Director, Student-Athlete Support Services, University of Utah**

"The CHAMPS program helped tremendously in my growth. Especially being an international student-athlete, I appreciated and utilized lots of the resources that were available. The concepts and principles in this book are as important now on tour as they were when I was in college. This book is perfect for recreational players to professional athletes. Muy bueno!" **Lorena Ochoa, Future's Tour Rookie/Player of the Year 2002, LPGA Tour**

"I would have loved to have had this book in my hands as a freshman. I was young, naive and not quite prepared for the academic and athletic rigors I was about to face. This book would have definitely helped me prepare for the challenges ahead. Becky Bell is a recognized leader in her field. Her wealth of personal insights and experiences add another dimension and make this book a must read for any student-athlete. I highly recommend it." **Steve Kerr, San Antonio Spurs, 4-Time NBA Champion**

Copyright 2003 by Becky Bell

This publication is designed to provide accurate and authoritative information with regard to the subject matter covered. Every attempt has been made to accurately transcribe quotations used in this book. In the event of a question arising about a quotation, we regret any error made and will be pleased to make the necessary correction in future editions. Some quotes have been edited for tense consistency, clarity and brevity.

Substantial discounts on bulk quantities of this book are available to corporations, professional associations, and other organizations. For details, contact the publisher.

NOTE: Due to NCAA compliance issues, using the names of current student-athletes is prohibited. The quotes are from student-athletes who attended the 2002 NCAA National Leadership Foundation Conference (Divisions 1,2 and 3), the national Student-Athlete Advisory Committees (SAAC), student-athletes nationally, and from former student-athletes.

Published by: The Game of Life
3675 W. Dawnbreaker Pl.
Tucson, Arizona 85745
Phone: (520) 743-7537
Fax: (520) 621-5337
bell@u.arizona.edu
www.u.arizona.edu/~bell

DEDICATION

IN MEMORY OF MY FATHER:
Edward Thomas Bell, Jr.
1926-1993

TO MY MOTHER:
Bobbie Jean Bell

AND

TO MY GODSON:
Cameron Omsberg

TABLE OF CONTENTS

Foreword

By Dr. Cedric Dempsey
Former NCAA President and Executive Director

It gives me great pleasure to write the foreword to this new and exciting book. As the executive director of the NCAA from 1994-2002, improving student-athlete welfare was one of my most important goals. I have seen the dramatic growth of Life Skills programs and the invaluable services and results it has provided over the years.

CHAMPS/Life Skills is designed for your growth, development and success in 5 areas: academics, athletics, personal development, career development and service. The main objectives we have set forth are as follows:

- To prepare student-athletes for leadership in a diverse and dynamic society.

- To enhance the collegiate experience of young men and women.

- To reinforce the values of fairness and integrity in intercollegiate athletics.

- To highlight the capacity of intercollegiate athletics to foster lifelong learning.

There are many opportunities for you to get involved in various activities and to experience things that can undoubtedly offer you a broader, more enriching, fulfilling, rewarding and satisfying experience at your college or university. We encourage you to do just that – get involved - challenge yourself in these areas - wander out of your comfort zone, stretch yourselves as students and as people, much like you do as athletes - to become the most complete, well-rounded person you can be – and ready for what life has to offer after graduation.

The stories that follow are from people who have been where you are. Some may actually be from your university. We are grateful to the "family" of student-athletes who were enthusiastic to share their experiences. Their stories are interesting, their advice heartfelt, and their comments worth considering. We hope that you will take away something that will help you in achieving your goals in these five areas.

Intercollegiate athletics can be a vehicle to teach life values and life skills. We hope that you will become involved in the CHAMPS/ Life Skills program at your university and will one day share your experiences with others. Enjoy the book and enjoy what CHAMPS/ Life Skills has to offer. Good luck to each and every one of you.

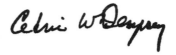

About the Author

Becky Bell has been the Director of C.A.T.S. Life Skills in the University of Arizona athletics department since 1997. She is a former student-athlete and All-American at UCLA (tennis), and also played one year of junior varsity basketball for the Bruins. After receiving her undergraduate degree in Kinesiology in 1981, she was an assistant tennis coach at UCLA for 5 years (including the 1981 National Championship, and 3 other Final Four appearances) before assuming the head coaching duties at the University of Arizona. 12 years at the helm resulted in two Regional Coach of the Year awards and 5 top-10 finishes for the Wildcats, including one Final Four. She has coached national champions and more than 25 All-Americans. She has also been a member of, and national coach for, the USTA (United States Tennis Association) Jr. Federation Cup teams and competed for a brief time professionally.

Becky earned her first Master's degree in Sports Administration in 1994 and her second Master's degree in Counseling (with an emphasis in Career Counseling) in 1997. She has made numerous national presentations and has spoken at many conferences and forums. She currently serves on the National 1A CHAMPS Board of Advisors.

Drawing on a very successful playing and coaching career, Becky brings more than 25 years of insights and experiences in intercollegiate athletics to this book.

Acknowledgements

I have said many times that there was ONE job that would have gotten me out of coaching, and being a Life Skills director was it. In my time with the C.A.T.S. Life Skills program, I have seen time and time again where CHAMPS/Life Skills has made a significant difference in the life of a student-athlete, and have heard similar stories from coordinators across the country. In hopes of sharing that inspiration with other student-athletes, I decided to write this book. There are numerous people to thank:

Thanks to the people who have given me the chance to do what I love: Gayle Godwin, Greg Hayes, Dr. Cedric Dempsey, Dr. Mary Roby, Jim Livengood and Rocky LaRose. Rocky, your strength and courage have been an inspiration to many.

To my former players, both at UCLA and the University of Arizona, who probably taught me more than I ever taught you. Special people, special times we've shared. Thank you for life long memories.

Thanks to all the student-athletes at the University of Arizona with whom I have had the distinct pleasure of working since taking over the C.A.T.S. Life Skills program.

Special thanks to Sue Sherburne, for your time, effort, input, positive energy and giving spirit. Sue, you have a way of making every person you meet feel special. The student-athletes at Penn St. are extremely lucky.

A HUGE thank you to Dr. Becky Ahlgren, and her staff at the NCAA. And most of all, I want to thank the student-athletes who were willing to share their stories and experiences and without whom this project would not have been possible.

Introduction

I know what you're thinking. Not another book telling me what to
do, and how to do it. Been there, done that. No thanks. Well, this
one's different. This one is by you, of you

> "The greatest
> thing in this
> world is not so
> much where we
> are, but in what
> direction we
> are moving."
>
> Oliver Wendell
> Holmes

and for you - the student-athlete. We have
asked hundreds of student-athletes from all
over the country what their secrets of success
were in the five CHAMPS/Life Skills areas of
academics, athletics, personal development,
career development and community service.
What follows are their personal stories
and experiences in each area – from their
struggles as a freshman, to their triumphs as
a senior, and everything in between.

It started as just an idea, really. You'd be
surprised at how something can develop
from an idea if you truly believe in its worth.
To be successful in anything, I think three
of the most important things you need are:
belief, commitment, and courage. A true belief in your abilities;
the commitment to achieve your goals; and the courage to work
through the challenging times. If you have a passion for what
you are doing, you are even luckier. This project has all of them.
There was no question I thought this could be an interesting and
worthwhile project. Life Skills coordinators across the country did.
The student-athletes we asked did. Coaches did. Hopefully, you
will too.

We produced a similar publication for our student-athletes at
Arizona that looked at the areas of academics, athletics and
personal development. It was read with a great deal of interest.
It was exciting to think that this could be applied to each of the
CHAMPS/Life Skills areas, and potentially help all student-athletes.
Using student-athletes from schools in all three divisions of the
NCAA, I also wanted to see the differences or similarities in their
experiences. Some things I anticipated. The willingness of those
who shared and the power of their stories, I never expected. It has
been incredibly inspiring to learn about, and to read about these
student-athletes' journeys.

There's a poster in my office. It's a picture of a beautiful autumn day, a path in a forest, with the word <u>DISCOVERY</u> framing the bottom, and the quote: "Two roads diverged in a wood and I – I took the one less traveled by, and that has made all the difference." (Robert Frost). I love this quote because I think it represents one of the best things about college. Some people know early on what they want to do. Most students don't. And that is what's so great - to be able to discover who you are and who you want to be. To discover what you want to do, and how you will accomplish it. To decide what road you want to take and what legacy you want to leave. It all starts here. It all starts now.

In my life, I've always drawn from the best coaches and teachers I have had. Think about the coaches and teachers you have had. What have you learned from them? How do you apply those things in your life? As a former coach, I found that one way to analyze success in athletics was to look at different aspects of the sport: the mental, physical, emotional, technical, and strategic components. Players could look at each area and analyze their strengths and weaknesses. I took the same approach for CHAMPS. I have found that success revolves around what I call P-Factor Analysis. If you analyze seven "P's": Personalization, Preparation, Process, Problem Solving, Persistence, Perspective and Pausing, you can begin to identify your strengths and things you can improve, that will ultimately lead you to greater success. We will examine P-Factor in depth in Chapter 2.

In coaching, I also encouraged my players to become students of the game. To learn as much as possible, then to apply what made sense to them. If they believed in what we were working on, and why we were doing that, it was easier to make progress and move forward. The same applies here. If you really believe in the value of life skills, and we hope you do, the more you will get out of it. This book encourages you to become students too...of life. We encourage you to be curious, ask questions, explore, learn, grow, and challenge yourself. Buy into what makes sense to you and get to work!

We will look briefly at the three "C's" of transition – changes, challenges and choices and at issues student-athletes face. What are they and how can you best deal with them? Each area of CHAMPS will present you with these, and every year you will be faced with them in some way, shape or form. Some may be more difficult than others. What will your changes, challenges and choices be? Wouldn't it be nice to know how others have gotten through? This book tells you. Following that, we will ask you to examine some of your long held beliefs. Are they true? Do you need to re-examine some of those beliefs? We'll take a look in the chapter on challenging your assumptions.

Then we get to what your peers have to say - student-athletes' advice, thoughts and insights for each area; things they would do differently, obstacles they've overcome, best thing they did in each area and lots more, including reasons for their success. There will be an assessment at the end of each section, where we will pose some broad, general questions and then some more specific ones with regard to P-Factor Analysis. Check and see if there are any patterns in your scores. Identify some focus areas. Finally, the "Game Plan" section is for you to jot down notes, ideas, and things you'd like to do or to try. We are not here to tell you what to do. You decide. You pick and choose. Because, just as CHAMPS/Life Skills defines five areas of commitment, **this is ultimately about one commitment – the commitment you make to yourself.**

Also, as you read this, I'd like to ask that you consider the totality of, and the relationships between, the components of CHAMPS – the parts and the whole, the art and the science, the logical and the imaginative, the right and the left. Again, think about the best coaches you have ever had. They knew the science of teaching your sport - the x's and o's, but they also knew the art of teaching it – of communicating, explaining, motivating, understanding, supporting, encouraging, of all the things you needed to become the best you could be. Think about how the CHAMPS areas relate to each other. How are they connected? Practicing your public speaking skills can help you in an interview. Taking a leadership role will help in numerous ways. The qualities you have as an athlete will transfer directly to the work world (discipline, work ethic, dedication, etc.) Much like pieces of a puzzle fit together, the same principle applies here. When all the pieces fit, you have success: within each area, and within the global concept of life skills. As a crew student-athlete explained, *"I feel more prepared to tackle challanges and achieve goals than ever before. My classes give me the knowledge, but athletics give me the interpersonal and leadership skills. From my summer internship, I can appreciate the fact that knowledge will get you nowhere if you do not have an understanding of teamwork, time management and communication."* Success in CHAMPS involves an interrelatedness and a connection between, and amongst, the areas. Be open to this connection. Look for the connection. Develop the connection.

Just as there are many skill requirements in your sport, each CHAMPS area also requires a certain skill set. Academic skills include having good study habits, note and test taking skills, writing skills, etc. In career development, they might be job related skills developed through internships, interviewing skills, presentation or researching skills. Doing a good job in community service requires good public speaking skills. One of the biggest skills that applies to all areas is communication skills. I can't think of too many general skills that are more important than communication skills. Communication is important when talking to professors, in writing papers, and in presenting ideas. It's critical in relationships. It's the difference between getting a job and not getting it. In fact, according to the National Association of Colleges and Employers (NACE), communication skills was listed as the number one quality employers look for in a candidate. How you dress even communicates something. There are obviously innumerable examples. We will ask you to identify skill sets necessary for success in each CHAMPS area and then to assess your individual abilities. **Just as in athletics, the more versatile you are, the more options you will have.**

Finally, I always find it interesting to see how student-athletes define themselves. In my experience, those student-athletes who have a broader self-concept and excel in more than just athletics, actually perform better, deal with stress and injuries better and have a more positive outlook on life than those whose identity is mainly as an athlete. Student-athletes we talked to agreed that they bounced back more quickly after a bad day, a bad practice, or a bad competition, if they had other things in their life to feel good about. One former softball player said, *"The idea of the "athlete identity" may become an issue if you view yourself ONLY as an athlete. It makes life harder when you become injured, are losing, or it is time to graduate. This is even more reason to stress a broader self-concept and a more balanced outlook on life - emphasizing the importance of a CHAMPS/Life Skills Program and all that it offers."* Phil Jackson, current head coach of the world champion Los Angeles Lakers and former coach of the

Chicago Bulls has said, "There's more to life than basketball. And there's more to basketball than basketball." Clearly, the more you have in your life, the better off you will be. While athletics may be a very big part of your life, remember it is just one part of who you are. What are some activities with which you might want to get involved to broaden your experience?

This is one of the major objectives of CHAMPS – to become well rounded and to have a balanced and diverse experience during your four or five years at college. The NCAA, in selecting their Woman of the Year, looks at three areas and weighs them equally: academics, athletics and personal development (including career development and community service). **They are all equally important.** The point is that extracurricular activities will make a difference, not only in one day getting a job or being accepted into graduate school, but in your overall growth and development and in your overall experience. I guarantee it.

You may not be excited by every single piece of advice in the book. That's fine. Keep reading. Because when something does click for you, when something does make sense, we encourage you to act on it. Identify the areas in which you would like to gain more knowledge, get involved or develop your skills. Identify resources and people who can help you. Make a note in the Game Plan section. Try this simple four-step approach:

- Utilize all available RESOURCES.
- Take advantage of, look for and create OPPORTUNITIES.
- Develop SKILLS and gain EXPERIENCE.
- Have OPTIONS.

Didn't this work for you as an athlete? You utilized your **resources** (parents, coaches, programs, teams, etc.) to build a solid foundation in your sport. You picked a college or university based on the one that gave you the most **opportunities** for success – in your sport, in school, and in other areas that were important to you. You developed certain **skills** and gained **experience**. Finally, you had **options** of which school to attend. The same approach applies in any facet of CHAMPS. Say, for example, you do five internships as one of our student-athletes at Arizona did. She utilized our resources, took advantage of the opportunities, developed skills and gained experience and had multiple (well-paying!) job offers when she graduated.

Another thing about this book is that it doesn't have to be read start to finish. You can read the chapters in any order, skip ahead to some, or come back later to others. You may want to read sections depending on what's going on in your life at a particular time. You are all at different places with different needs – and those needs will change. This book isn't rocket science – but we do want you to give serious consideration to what your fellow student-athletes are sharing with you. The idea is to be open to new experiences and to make lifestyle choices. We don't want this to be a part-time thing. We want this to become a part of who, and what, you become. Don't underestimate the power you have in creating your future – even at this stage in your life. One diver summed it up best: *"College is about learning. It's more than just learning what is being taught in your gen-ed classes. It's about learning how to listen, how to think… how to achieve and how to communicate. It's about learning what kind of person you are and what kind of person you want to be. It's about learning how to live."*

Henry Ford once said, "There isn't a man living who isn't capable of doing more than he thinks he can do." Consider your unique skills, abilities, knowledge and wisdom – what ARE you capable of achieving? No matter where you are on your journey, you can achieve great things. I believe that. I hope you all reach your dreams. But I assure you, what you will get by reaching those dreams will not be nearly as important as the person you become along the way.

NOTE: CHAMPS/Life Skills and CHAMPS are used interchangeably throughout the book. If your school does not have a CHAMPS/Life Skills program, or if you are not yet in college, look for the resources you do have available – coaches, teachers, counselors, advisors, student services, counseling centers, teaching/learning centers, career centers, the internet, etc. The concept and philosophy of CHAMPS is just as important before college as it is in college. You may also want to look up the websites of the schools listed in the back of this book. On these sites are links to numerous resources in each of the areas.

CHAMPS/
Life Skills
Overview

Academics

Athletics

Personal Development

Career Development

Community Service

CHAMPS/Life Skills Overview

The CHAMPS/Life Skills program focuses on five commitments that are meant to enhance the quality of the student-athlete experience within the university setting. The emphasis is on the development of the total person and meeting their needs in each of these areas.

Commitment to Academic Excellence

Supporting the academic progress and opportunities for student-athletes to excel in their chosen field of study and toward intellectual development and graduation.

Commitment to Athletic Excellence

Providing programs that are based on a commitment to sportsmanship, equity, fair play and integrity and dedicated to the well-being of each and every student-athlete. Providing facilities, coaching staffs and support services that will enable student-athletes to excel. This area includes strength and conditioning and medical services.

Commitment to Personal Development

Supporting the development of a well-balanced and healthy lifestyle for student-athletes, encouraging emotional well-being, personal growth and decision-making skills. The main areas include health and wellness, leadership and character and essential life skills.

Commitment to Career Development

Placing a priority on preparing for life after college. This includes examining interests, abilities and values and includes resume writing, interviewing skills, job search strategies, graduate school admissions assistance and more. The idea is to have a broad based experience and to develop transferable skills toward a rewarding career and productive lifestyle.

Commitment to Service

Encouraging student-athletes to give back to the campus and surrounding communities. Embracing a chance to make a difference and to develop the foundation for a lifelong commitment of service.

The CHAMPS/Life Skills program at your school exists to help you create balance in your life now, and to be successful long after you leave your university. This balance will be by design: your design. You create it and you will live it. It is an investment in your future. You are encouraged to make that investment and that commitment to excellence on a day-to-day basis in each of the five areas.

Every year at our new student-athlete orientation, I am amazed. Not by the amount of athletic talent in the room, but by the potential - for expression, creativity and achievement - outside of athletics. It's there, waiting to be explored, discovered and pursued. You all have what it takes to succeed in these areas. If you are willing to apply the same qualities that it took to achieve success in your sport, you can achieve success in all areas of CHAMPS/Life Skills.

P-Factor Analysis Overview

Personalization

Preparation

Process

Problem Solving

Persistence

Perspective

Pausing

P-Factor Analysis Overview

As I mentioned earlier, in athletic competition, there are mental, physical, emotional, strategic and technical aspects in any event. If you win or lose, many times, the win or loss can be traced to how you performed on that day, in those areas. In studying the elements of success for CHAMPS, I have narrowed it down to seven "P's" that, when analyzed, can determine your strengths and weaknesses, and present you with a guideline to approaching CHAMPS. We will be hearing from student-athletes where P-Factor made a significant difference in their achievements on the field and in their experiences off of it. They may call them different things, but most of their definitions can easily fit into one or more of the "P's". P-Factor Analysis includes: Personalization, Preparation, Process, Problem Solving, Persistence, Perspective, and Pausing. Let's take a close look at each one.

Personalization

"In reading the lives of great men, I found that the first victory they won was over themselves. Self discipline with all of them came first."

President Harry Truman

The most important relationship you will ever have is with yourself. Let me repeat that: **The most important relationship you will ever have is with yourself.** In addition, the relationship you have with yourself will determine the relationship you have with others. You've heard it a million times. Let's make it a million and one! You are 100% responsible for yourself, your life and the consequences of your choices. Bottom line? You choose what happens to you. Are you doing your best to fully accept that responsibility?

Sounds simple, but we know it's not. We've all heard about the angel on one shoulder and the devil on the other. One is telling you what you know you should do and the other one is tempting you with the wrong choice. It happens every day, in many situations: academics, (attending class), athletics (going the extra mile in workouts or conditioning), attitudes (being positive), social choices (being responsible), and you can probably think of many more examples. Think of the ones that affect you on a daily basis. Who is winning that battle?

You may be faced with making some decisions that could impact your life dramatically and for many years to come. These **defining moments** happen in all of our lives. When are your defining moments? Just as it's easier to blow things off once you do it the first time, it's also easier to maintain a commitment if you stay focused on achieving your goals. Those who are truly committed to success put themselves and their goals first and make that daily commitment to excellence. What DO you want? What IS your purpose? What ARE your goals and values? **What percentage of how you live is congruent with those goals and values?** Can you identify the things (circumstances, people, or attitudes) that move you towards your goals or lead you away from them? One student-athlete commented, *"As a freshman, you get thrown into a whole new world with lots of new opportunities and losing sight of who you are is your demise. Remember your goals, your character, your upbringing. It will carry you through."*

Much like a bank account, the more you put in, the more you have over time. Are you making a deposit or a withdrawal in yourself every day in these areas? Are you better today than yesterday? You didn't get to be a good athlete overnight. You have devoted a tremendous amount to your athletic pursuits. How about the other areas? Lots of people just want to stay in their comfort zone and are afraid to challenge themselves. They'll just stay where they are, with what they have. Have you ever really thought about why you do, or don't do, certain things? There is a reason – it's because, at whatever level and for whatever reason, it works for you. Are you protecting yourself or afraid of confronting or trying something? What issues are you dealing with and are they the real issues? To whom do you give power in making decisions about what happens to you? Is your motivation more internal or external? Why DO you do the things that you do? Real and lasting change occurs only when you give yourself that power. You have to be willing to trade that safety and security for something more meaningful and significant in your life in order to reach your true potential.

The first habit in Steven Covey's *The 7 Habits of Highly Effective People* (1989) is: **Be Proactive.** Being proactive is at the very core of life skills. By taking control and creating your own experience, you are determining what happens to you. Are you taking the initiative to make things happen, or just reacting to what does happen? The first three habits, in fact, are all in the area of personalization: Be proactive; Begin with the end in mind; and Put first things first. (For the other habits, see page 98).

All of this leads us to one of the most often repeated pieces of advice from the student-athletes: SET GOALS. Many people like the SMARTEST method of goal setting:

Short and long term goals; Measurable goals; Achievement strategies to reach goals; Realistic goals; Time-bound goals; Exhibit your goals; Seek support for your goals; Target obstacles to achieving your goals. (Check with your CHAMPS coordinator for more information on this or other goal setting methods.)

By setting short and long term goals, you can identify exactly what you want the end result to be, as well as each step along the way. What needs to happen first? Then what? What are your strategies to achieve them? What are you willing to sacrifice? Make a firm commitment to your plan and gain some momentum by accomplishing smaller goals first. As one 3-sport athlete said, *"Set goals. Every decision you make, you should refer to your list of goals and ask yourself: Can this help or hinder achieving the goals I have set in place?"* Over time, and little by little, you will get there.

You all have unique gifts and talents. While some skills and traits can be developed and improved over time, you also have some **personal preferences** that are essentially an innate part of who you are, and what your make up is. Knowing and understanding some of these preferences, such as personality types, and learning styles, can guide you in developing an individualized approach to CHAMPS that can increase your chances for success. The Myers-Briggs Type Inventory looks at preferences in four different areas: (introversion/extroversion (how you are energized); intuition/sensing (how you take in and process information); thinking/feeling (how you make decisions) and judging/perceiving (what kind of lifestyle you prefer) and measures sixteen psychological types. It can be used and applied in many different situations, including career choices and understanding relationships.

Learning styles can also be identified. Discovering your style can help you maximize what you learn. You can apply that knowledge in class, when you study and when you take exams. Styles are divided into three main types. Visual (you learn best through seeing); Auditory (you learn best through hearing); and Kinesthetic (you learn best through doing). Each of these types asks questions, gathers information, learns and discovers meaningful answers in different ways. For example, in your sport, do you learn best if:

- Your coach explains something to you verbally?
- They demonstrate it so you can see it?
- You just do it and "feel it" kinesthetically?

How might this apply to your academic endeavors? As with the Myers-Briggs, although we have all of the types in us, we usually have a preference in one of the areas. Matching learning styles with teaching styles can prove to be extremely beneficial. Check with your CHAMPS coordinator for both Myers-Briggs and learning style assessments.

The importance of self-efficacy (your belief about what you can accomplish) is often overlooked. Do you ever consider how confident you are in situations other than athletics? You are a confident, self-assured athlete when competing. How about if you need to speak with a professor? Present something in class? Go for a job interview? How might you apply the same level of confidence you have in your sport to other aspects of your life? In identifying some of the critical issues they face today, student-athletes listed self-esteem as one. Nathaniel Branden in *The Six Pillars of Self Esteem* (1994), has listed the following as pillars of self-esteem: The practice of *living consciously*; the practice of *self-acceptance*; the practice of *self-responsibility*; the practice of *self-assertiveness*; the practice of *living purposefully* and the practice of *personal integrity*. I won't go into these in detail, but these pillars are all essential and necessary life skills!

Pride can also play a role. Pride can be a good thing but it can sometimes get in the way. Have you ever not admitted that you were wrong because of your pride? Not gotten help or not asked a question in class because you thought it was a dumb question? I have. Trust me, speaking from experience, once you get the courage to ask the questions, it really does get easier. Plus, at least 10 other people in the class probably have the same question! Don't let pride be about appearances rather than what it should be about - real growth.

Develop habits now that will pay off later. One volleyball player said it best: *"Get priorities straight and stick to them. This may be college right now and seem unimportant but life lessons and habits are learned here, so start NOW!!"*

Preparation

> *"If I had six hours to chop down a tree, I'd spend the first four hours sharpening the axe."*
>
> President
> Abraham Lincoln

Quick question: Who out there among you, woke up one day and you were a great athlete? Just rolled out of bed one Saturday and you were the best? Obviously, it doesn't happen that way. It takes time, lots and lots of hard work, practice... preparation! **Preparation is the foundation upon which everything else is built.** It begins with planning and implementing the strategies you have identified to achieve your goals and developing the skills it will require to get there. It means preparation for the day-to-day tasks and preparation for the future.

Bottom line – where are you, where do you want to go, and how will you get there? Will you be better or worse a week, month or year from now because you won't be the same? You know as well as I do that there are no short cuts. The number one reason for success stated by the student-athletes: HARD WORK. You don't go into the biggest competition of the year by practicing ten hours or lifting five hours the day before – why would you do that for tests, career planning, leadership development or anything else? If you are well prepared, your chances for success in anything are exponentially greater. Success is about a person's confidence at any moment in time, as much as their ability. If you have done everything you possibly can to be ready for something, aren't you also more confident? That confidence may end up making the difference by giving you that extra mental edge when it counts the most.

You have to be committed to your goals and know what your priorities are. Absolutely everything you do should have a purpose. It's been said that goals determine priorities and priorities determine if you will reach your goals. Think about that. Makes sense doesn't it? What are your biggest priorities and do your daily activities reflect that? I like the analogy Covey uses of putting rocks in a bucket. You have "x" amount of big rocks, and "x" amount of little rocks. When you try to put the little rocks in first, the big ones won't fit later. But if you put the big ones in first, you can then fit the little ones in around them. Are you taking care of your biggest, most important rocks (priorities) first? Your purpose must be clear and you must be clear – about what you want, how important it is to you and how committed you are to achieving it. Some of the things you will hear time and time again, in the advice that follows, are to prioritize, to stay true to yourself and to be focused on your vision.

One of the overwhelming challenges student-athletes face is time management. You will notice that as a theme throughout the five areas. **In order to manage your time, you have to manage yourself.** You have to know your priorities. Advice from the student-athletes? Use a planner. Be organized. Use little blocks of time. Don't procrastinate. One soccer player suggested, *"Plan your day out specifically by writing it down in a planner, especially when you will do your homework. Seeing your whole day mapped out in front of you is so much less stressful because you are more organized."* It's great advice. Figure out today what you want to accomplish tomorrow. Take 5-10 minutes every night so you can hit the ground running tomorrow. Anticipate what will happen. What is your schedule? When will you eat? When will you study? What HAS to get done? What are your priorities? What are you willing to commit to (short-term and long-term) to be prepared? When you read the "Best Thing I Did For Myself" quotes in each section you'll notice that many of these "best practices" are about preparation! Most of you are willing to go the extra mile in your sport – outside practice, lessons, conditioning, lifting, etc. Go the extra mile in the other CHAMPS areas and be prepared…for your future and for life.

"The journey of a thousand miles starts with a single step."

Chinese Proverb

Process

The first component in Kouzes-Posner's model of leadership (used at the NCAA Leadership Conference) is: **Challenge the Process.** Your process can be short-term (doing a drill in practice) or it can be long-term (learning a new skill or trying to reach a long-term goal). Just because something has been done one way in the past doesn't necessarily mean that's the way it should always be done. What's working and what's not working for you? Is there a better way of doing it? As one golfer stated, *"There is not one single champion that does things the way others do them. Every person has their own way to do things. If you want to be different, you have to act differently and think differently."*

Many tangible and intangible factors go into making something successful – the things you do on a day-to-day basis, paying attention to detail, being thorough, etc. **Your daily process, impacts your ultimate success as much as any other single factor.** Instead of thinking about the outcome, think about the fundamentals, the details, and the steps that will put you in a position to succeed. Student-athletes agreed. One volleyball player said, *"Try to focus on the process and the steps to success, instead of worrying too much about the outcome."* If you are consistently taking care of the little things - the process - day in and day out, the big things will take care of themselves.

If preparation is the "what", the process is the "how". For example, if your goal is to study every day, to be prepared for exams, what is your process? Do you study in a quiet place where you can concentrate? Is your mind fresh? Do you eliminate distractions - or do you study in a loud dorm room, answer the phone every 5 minutes, talk to your neighbors when they come over, and study on commercial breaks of your favorite TV show?! **You need to put yourself in the environment most conducive to getting the results you want.**

You also need to be consistent in your process. Develop the right habits. Consistency in the fundamentals of your daily routines will mean consistency in your "performances". If someone is practicing a serve in tennis, and the toss needs to be in a particular place to hit the serve correctly, if that toss is inconsistent, the serve will be inconsistent. Understanding the process will also allow you to figure things out on your own much better, since you'll have some checkpoints and know exactly what you should be doing.

Besides hard work, setting goals, and time management, another top reason for student-athletes' success was focus. Your focus should be on the present task. How can you concentrate on what you should be if you're thinking about what might happen in the future, what has happened in the past, or what you're having for dinner that night?! Your focus needs to be on what you are doing NOW, your process NOW. Are you just "involved in" or are you "committed to" what you are doing? Dr. Jim Loehr, renowned sports psychologist, says you need to be **fully engaged** in what you are doing – physically energized, emotionally connected, mentally focused and spiritually aligned to have the best chance for success at that moment and to fulfill your destiny as an athlete. Are you fully engaged in what you are doing?

There are also different types of focus. The type of focus you need will depend on the situation and is based on 2 main dimensions: broad/narrow (the amount of information you need to deal with) and internal/external (the source of information and the direction of your focus). You may need your focus to be broad/internal (picking where to serve in tennis) or broad/external (point guard running a fast break); a narrow/external one (hitting a putt); or narrow/internal (being calm). What cues are most relevant for your tasks at a given point in time? Stay in the present and have your focus in the appropriate place.

Another interesting thing we did was to ask the student-athletes if they had it to do all over again, what would they do differently? In other words, how would their process change? Each area will show the main things they said they would do differently given another chance. Learning is all a part of the process. Things are gained and lost along the way, but we hope these insights will assist you with your process and help you to avoid some unnecessary pitfalls.

By analyzing P-Factor, we will be able to examine your process. If you take some time in the assessment section and really analyze each "P" Factor, with each CHAMPS area, you should get a pretty good idea of your overall profile. You've set your goals. What you do on a daily basis - your process - will determine if you'll reach those goals. You've heard the quote, "Success is a journey, not a destination." The journey is the process.

> *"The ultimate measure of a man is not where he stands in the moment of comfort and convenience, but where he stands in time of challenge and controversy."*
>
> Martin Luther King

Problem Solving

Problem solving can be the difference between success and failure. Problems bring out character, courage and creativity. You are constantly faced with solving problems. Some may be within yourself; some may involve others. Every day you have to figure something out, right? What are your skills and resources? Who is your support system? I have found many times that for every adversity, there is an equal or greater benefit. Sometimes you just have to look for it.

In my experience, people who are optimistic and have a positive attitude deal with life's problems better through resiliency, flexibility and adaptability. In fact, student-athletes listed "attitude" as one of their top reasons for success. In his book *Learned Optimism* (1990), Dr. Martin Seligman says people who are optimistic view problems as temporary, specific, and impersonal. People who are pessimistic see problems as permanent, pervasive and personal. The opposite explanations hold true for explaining good things that happen. How do you handle problems? Does a problem in one area affect everything you do? Do you see it as temporary or long lasting? Do you personalize it? In general, would you consider yourself more of an optimist or a pessimist?

Being positive includes how you carry yourself. If your body language is positive, it says you are confident and in charge. Think about the unspoken message you send if you are walking tall and confidently, versus slouching, whining, or moping. If you are negative, have you ever considered the impact that your negativity may have? How much energy is wasted and NOT given to the task at hand? What attitude and messages do you send when you compete? Speak to a group or a professor? Interview? What about when you win or lose? Let your unspoken messages be positive ones of confidence and poise.

The past can sometimes be the best predictor of the future. Think about your problem solving skills/history and consider the following:

- How do past situations affect you today?
- Are there certain patterns for you when it comes to problem solving?
- Can you critically analyze a situation? Are you asking the right questions and attacking the right problem?
- Do you have all the facts?
- What are your options?

Look at the quotes in each component on "Obstacles We Overcame" and you will see how these student-athletes solved some of their problems. Here's one example: *"Study habits – I didn't have any! My high school was somewhat easy – meaning I didn't have to study outside the classroom. So I had to learn how to find time to sit and do and read the homework. I did poorly in a class that required a lot of reading, so it opened my eyes."*

If you are struggling in one of the areas of CHAMPS, let's figure out why. Which of the P-Factors are holding you back? If you are not getting the results you want, maybe it's not a matter of trying harder, but trying smarter. Maybe you don't need more quantity of time, but quality of time. Maybe you don't need to think more, but to think less and trust your preparation more (assuming you're prepared!). Of course you need to evaluate what you are doing, but those who think TOO much sometimes suffer from what we call "paralysis by analysis". Competition has, in many ways, prepared you well to deal with problems because if you can do it on the field or court, you can do it in life. **Good competitors are good problem solvers.** They welcome it, in fact. The tougher the situation, the tougher they are. Do you think Michael Jordan ever backed down from a problem? Jordan was at his BEST when the problems were the WORST. Controlling your emotional response to a problem goes a long way in solving it. Michael was calm, cool and collected under pressure. This emotional control was a big part of his competitive advantage. How well do you control your emotions – in and out of your sport?

Stress can certainly play a role. 96% of Arizona student-athletes that we surveyed thought that they had more stress in their life than general students. Do you agree? How do you deal with stress?

What triggers stress for you? Dr. Loehr believes that stressors, or as he calls them "storms", are the most powerful stimulus for personal growth and development. The trick is learning how to use them to your advantage. He believes that the stronger you are as a person and the deeper your roots in the fundamental dimensions of the physical, emotional, mental and spiritual (i.e. the true spirit for what you are doing), the better you can deal with stress. Translation: DEVELOP LIFE SKILLS! Develop your capacity in those areas and see what a difference it can make. If you find stress is affecting you in unhealthy ways, let your support system or other available resources help you.

A person's **character** can be instrumental in how they approach and solve problems. Legendary coach John Wooden has said, "Be more concerned with your character than with your reputation. Your character is who you really are, while your reputation is merely who others think you are." The organization CHARACTER COUNTS!₅ₘ (www.charactercounts.org) lists the following as the Six Pillars of Character₅ₘ: **trustworthiness, respect, responsibility, fairness, caring, and citizenship.** (See also, Pursuing Victory with Honor on the same website.) Similarly, the NCAA has a value statement for their Education Outreach Services staff that states the following: "Our character... rests on four qualities: the **respect** we show one another; the **cooperation** we give one another; the **communication** we have with one another; and the **commitment** we dedicate to one another. The **excellence** of our product finds its foundation here. Together we form a **unity** far larger and more effective than the sum of our individual efforts." All of these ideas, if they reflect values you have, can be applied to your teams, to relationships, and certainly to problem solving. What kind of character do you have?

Remember your CHAMPS/Life Skills support staff is there to help. A track and field athlete concurred: *"Trust the people who are here to help you. Remember, that if you have a problem, what they tell you and what they advise you, is part of the solution."* To be successful in anything you need to be a good problem solver. P-Factor Analysis may be a good way to identify areas to work on and problems to solve!

Persistence

> *"Dogged persistence is the root of success. Never give up and never give in."*
>
> Author unknown

Matt Muehlebach (Men's Basketball University of Arizona, Final Four 1988) tells the story of when he arrived on campus as a highly recruited basketball player. He was sure he was the next superstar out of the UA program. Pick up games were show time for him. As he tells it, "Future NBA stars were nothing." Bring it on. By the time real practice started, Matt was praying for a season ending injury so he wouldn't have to play! It was that bad. It was that hard. He was in over his head (he thought). But Matt was patient and worked harder than anyone. His time came. He helped lead the Wildcats to their first Final Four appearance. His story is the epitome of persistence, of hanging in there, of believing that he could do it.

Understand that things take time. As Matt found out, they may even get worse before they get better. Be patient, but be determined. Have courage, discipline, belief, and an unwavering commitment – even if there is an occasional step backwards. If you have a true passion for something, persistence will come naturally. Things may not happen overnight, but they will over time. All of us have struggled with confidence at one time or another. Stay positive and keep believing. One student-athlete said the best thing she ever did was, *"stuck out the hard times (mostly as a freshman) and endured, persisted…now I am in a position of influence (team captain) and can really make a difference."* Successful athletes, or people who are successful in any field, don't just quit when the going gets tough. True competitors embrace adversity and find a way to work through it. It makes them smarter, stronger and tougher the next time around. How much of a true competitor are you?

Resilience, and how you deal with setbacks, is a critical determinant in a person's success. How quickly can you come back from a failure or disappointment? It's been said that **where there is no faith in the future, there is no power in the present.** You have to continue when you become discouraged, as hard as that sometimes is, because only through perseverance will you succeed. The greater the goal, the greater the commitment needed to achieve it. As we all know, if it were easy, everyone could do it. Author Richard Kipling once said, "If you don't get what you want, it is a sign either that you did not seriously want it or that you tried to bargain for the price." There is a price to be paid for anything worth achieving. The price of success, many times, is persistence. Many successful people, probably most successful people, failed before they succeeded.

"A mind once stretched by a new idea never goes back to its original dimensions."

Oliver Wendell Holmes

Perspective

One of the biggest lessons my dad ever taught me was to not get too excited with winning and not too disappointed about losing. To keep it in perspective because there was always another match to play. One of my favorite quotes is from a soccer player: *"Don't let success get in your head and don't let failure get in your heart."* Without question, the lessons that athletics can teach us are invaluable. Even Tiger Woods has said, "Golf has been good to me, but the lessons I've learned have transcended the game."

My dad also once told me that you could learn something from any situation. It was up to me to give the best I could, and no matter what the situation, learn something from it. Think of a time you were disappointed. Now rethink it – is there something positive you could have taken away from it? Here's a great quote from one football player who began his career as a walk-on and wound up earning a scholarship: *"Looking back on it, I was glad to have started as a walk-on. It gave me great perspective. I had the experience of a full scholarship football player and that of a non-recruited player. It helped me to fully understand the variety of experiences that student-athletes face."*

We all know there are 2 sides to every story. The same is true of perspectives. Have you ever seen those pictures or paintings where, depending on how you look at it, you can see different things? There's one picture, where if you look at it one way, you see a tired old lady; if you look at it another way, you see a beautiful young woman. Same picture, different perspectives. You choose how you want to view circumstances. The exact same situation can be viewed positively or negatively. You can either tell yourself, "Geez, it's really cold and windy today, we're on the road, I'm exhausted, we're not supposed to win anyway…" Or you can say, "What a great chance to get a win, we've worked hard, we're prepared, excited, and can't wait to get out there." Again, same situation, different perspective. Consider the following for yourself:

- What is your frame of reference (through which filters do you see the world)?
- When you face a difficult situation, do you see "obstacles" or "challenges"?
- Do you see the big picture, or just the immediate situation?
- How does your perspective relate to problem solving?
- What do you see as things you can control?
- How well do you deal with change, uncertainty, and ambiguity?
- How can your goals affect your perspective?

Understanding personality types can provide very useful information and help with problem solving as well. This assessment is revealing in numerous ways. It helps you to understand yourself, but it also helps you to understand, appreciate and accept others. How accepting are you of differences? Consider how different your perspective might be if: You were a different gender or race? You grew up in another part of the country or in another country? Your family make-up was different? You were born 25, or even 50, years earlier? You had more money or less money? See if looking at things from a different perspective changes your viewpoint.

Perspective also changes with time and experience. The first time you were in a big game situation, perhaps with the game on the line, was probably much different than after you had been in that same situation 10 or 20 times. The more experience you have at something, the better you will be at it and the less overwhelming and intimidating the situation will appear to be. Similarly, the more job interviews you do, the more public speaking, the more times you talk to a professor, the more comfortable and confident you will be! When faced with an emotional or difficult decision, time and distance may also help your perspective. Sometimes it's better to wait a day or two before making a decision. That time and distance can sometimes provide a more clear and rational viewpoint. Many student-athletes have to deal with injuries during their career. Sometimes they will come back with a different perspective on their sport (or life). Have you had an incident in your life that has changed your perspective?

Sports psychologists will tell you that what you say to yourself is critical and that there is actually a physiological response. That's why so many Olympic athletes practice visualization. Much like learning an athletic movement, and the repetition needed for muscle memory, your brain can also be trained. What do you tell yourself about your potential in the CHAMPS areas? When you know why you're doing something, and believe in it, it makes a difference in how you view it doesn't it? Remember, it's your perception and interpretation of the situation, not necessarily the situation itself, that is the most important thing. It's been said that life is 10% of what happens to you and 90% of how you deal with it. Stay positive, focused and remember the big picture.

Pausing

"Learn from the past; enjoy the present; envision the future."

Author unknown

Taking some time for yourself is a must. Maybe it's taking time to reenergize, refocus, appreciate or reflect. One football player commented, *"Take time to reflect on the experience while it is happening. Appreciate the opportunity. Play your sport with the joy of your childhood."* We all need time for ourselves. Be aware of when those times are. Schedule them if you have to. Maybe you can use the time walking to class, driving home at night, writing in a journal, connecting with your spiritual side, or listening to your favorite music. Take advantage of breaks during the day. But make sure you are getting the time you need for you. Just like you need physical recovery time in your sport, you need mental and emotional recovery time as well. This will be different for everyone but it is an important piece of the puzzle. There are lots of things to take care of every day. Make sure one of those things is YOU.

Mike Candrea, softball coach at Arizona drives almost an hour every day to school and then an hour back home at night. He's been doing this for 17 years! One day I asked him, "Aren't you tired of that drive, doesn't it get OLD?!" He told me he loves it – in the morning, on the way in, he can plan the day and at night he uses the time for reflection and relaxation. What outlets do you have to relieve the stress and re-energize?

We will be applying the principles of P-Factor to CHAMPS/ Life Skills: academics, athletics, personal development, career development and community service. Remember, at the end of each section is an assessment to see how you are doing in each area and a "Game Plan" for you to take notes.

The Three "C's"

Changes

Being away from home

New environment

Challenges

Academics

Time management

Athletics

Choices

Support system

Circle of influence

The Three "C's"
Changes, Challenges and Choices

At our new student-athlete orientation we discuss the three "C's" of transitions: Changes, Challenges and Choices. We ask our freshmen to write down what their biggest concerns are for the upcoming year. Not surprisingly, some are changes (being away from home, making new friends), some are challenges (academics, playing time) and some are choices (staying true to themselves, going to class every day, etc.). Changes, challenges and choices also come into play at the end of your college career. Many of you will be leaving your sport after many, many years of participation and dedication. How will you deal with that "loss" in your life? With what will you replace it? What might your changes, challenges and choices be when you graduate? This is an extremely difficult time for many athletes. It's worth thinking about before that day comes and it's how your CHAMPS/Life Skills program can play an instrumental role.

Changes

For freshmen students, the changes are numerous: Living away from home, bigger classes, new environment, new roommate, new teammates, new coaches, etc. Your professors may not know you by name anymore. You were a big fish in high school. You're now in a stream with lots of big fish. You are now responsible for getting to class, managing your money, eating the right foods, doing your laundry....lots of stuff like that! At times it can seem overwhelming. The good news? You don't need to feel alone – lots of people are going through the same things. The better news? Your life skills program, or university's student services, has many support services for you if you need them. Just ASK!

Challenges

The challenges sometimes are even more dramatic: academics will be harder (grades normally drop 1 grade from what you got in high school and the recommended study time is 3 hours of studying for every hour of class), athletics is more demanding, everyone wants something from you, managing your time is difficult, trying to eat the proper foods and get the proper rest can be tough, and there are many more. Your immediate support system (family) may not be right there anymore. You may get homesick or feel lonely and depressed. Stress levels may increase.

While many of these may be more immediate challenges, another challenge many face today is that of perceptions. Billy Mills, Gold Medalist in the 10,000 meters (1964 Olympics), and Native American, says the biggest challenge we face in today's changing world is that of perceptions. Think of perceptions people may have based on race, gender, socioeconomic status, athletic accomplishments, or other factors. What battles have you faced because of perceptions?

The challenges are many, and that is why knowing what resources are available and using them is critical! We will ask you to identify both campus and athletic department resources at the end of each CHAMPS section.

Choices

Choices are really where the rubber meets the road. Let's face it – change is inevitable, growth is optional. You will always face changes and challenges – but what choices will you make? Will you ask for help if you need it? Will you speak up if you should? Will you have the strength of character to live by your values? What will you do in those defining moments we talked about? As one student-athlete said, *"Make responsible decisions. It only takes one mistake to jeopardize something special."* I've heard it said that courage is the first of human qualities, because it is the quality that guarantees all others. Do you have the courage to make the tough, but right, decisions?

Aside from your athletic team, there are two other "teams" that you will choose, that will play a huge role in your success. The first of these teams is your **support system**. Building a support system can be one of the most important things you will ever do. Identify the people who can help you – mentors, family, friends, teammates, coaches – anyone who will support and guide you, remind you of your goals and help keep you on track. They may be different people for different areas, but make sure that you have a solid support team in place!

The second "team" is your **circle of influence.** The people with whom you associate help determine who you are today, and who you will be in four or five years. Who is your "team" of influence? Associate with people who will be positive influences and can help you get to where you want to go. One basketball player said simply, *"Surround yourself with good people and good things will happen to you."*

At recent NCAA Foundation National Leadership Conferences, at regional leadership conferences, and when we surveyed student-athletes, they have identified the following as challenges they face. As you read through them, which ones are current issues for you?

- Time management
- Academic issues (study skills, test taking skills, major choices)
- Adjustment to college life
- Self esteem
- Nutrition
- Dietary supplements
- Steroids
- Eating disorders/Body image issues
- Alcohol and substance abuse
- Sexual responsibility/Awareness
- Sexual orientation
- Stress management
- Adequate sleep
- Grief and loss
- Diversity education/awareness
- Relationship issues
- Campus/student safety
- Date rape
- Sexual harassment
- Sport and gender equity – Title IX
- Violence and crime
- Public perception of student-athletes/Negative media
- Financial issues/Money management
- Career planning
- Campus/community support
- Cohesive student-athlete community
- Gambling
- Student-athlete integration and socialization

- Coach or team issues
- Hazing
- Health and Wellness issues
- Spiritual Guidance
- NCAA Rules
- Minority issues
- Discrimination
- Depression
- Respect – for yourself and others
- The trust gap between student-athletes and coaches administrators
- Summer/voluntary workouts
- The recruiting process
- Time demands
- Perceived manipulation of student-athletes

Your life skills support staff is always there for you and can assist you with any of these issues. Remember that. Utilize them. The goal is for you to have what you need to be successful across the board. I have seen so many student-athletes be afraid to admit how they really feel, what's really going on with them, what they really need. Listen – everyone struggles. You are not alone. Here's what your fellow student-athletes will tell you: One – do not be afraid to ask for help. Two – build a strong support system (and positive circle of influence). Three – utilize the resources available to you. If you do these things you can, and will, get through just about anything. **As long as you have the power to choose, you have the power to succeed.**

Challenging Your Assumptions

Act on
your inspirations

Be realistic

Don't settle
for mediocrity

Be unafraid to take risks

Have a "PLAN B"

Challenging Your Assumptions

We all have assumptions. In my opinion, your assumptions about your abilities, or whether you believe you can succeed is one of the most important factors in whether or not you actually will succeed. Do you think you can do it or not? You also need to be realistic. What we're going to try to get you to do in this chapter is: CHALLENGE YOUR ASSUMPTIONS.

Pat Summitt, head basketball coach at the University of Tennessee and winner of 6 national championships was interviewed a few years ago on 60 Minutes. Coach Summitt is known for pushing her players, being demanding and having very high expectations. When questioned about her approach she simply said, **"Why would you want to be mediocre?"** I love that. Exactly. Why would you want to be mediocre? Why would you ever NOT want to be the best you possibly could. Seems obvious, but how many people do you know that never reach their potential?

You all have things you believe about what you can achieve. These might be fixed beliefs. Unfortunately, sometimes they might even be limiting beliefs. Maybe you haven't received the proper amount of encouragement or guidance. In some cases, it's because people just don't believe in what they can achieve. Others haven't tried or they haven't been challenged. Whatever the case, forget all that for now and test if what you think is really true. There isn't a student-athlete yet, with whom I have worked, that I didn't truly believe in their potential. But YOU need to believe in your potential and capabilities. I've heard it said that 80% of all obstacles come from within. Can you identify the things holding you back?

You've probably all seen the movie Jerry Maguire. Well, think about an assumption you have about yourself. O.K., show me... the EVIDENCE! If ten of your peers and closest friends were asked, would they, being completely honest, agree with your assessment? Is it in your best interests in the long run, and for your future, to hold on to those thoughts and attitudes? Are you maybe, just maybe, selling yourself short in any area? Are you doing what you're doing today just because it's what you did yesterday or because of someone else's expectations? Most of you have no problem articulating where you think you can go with your sport.

How about academics, your career or what you could mean in the lives of children in the community? How far CAN you go? Here's how one sports writer described Tiger Woods many years ago, when he was first breaking onto the professional scene. "For all the things that strike you about this prodigy, this is the one that separates him from the rest…Tiger Woods is not afraid to win. A lot of them are you know. At the moment of truth, they back off. It may be subconscious. Or not. But winning isn't nearly as easy as it appears. It requires a great deal more than most of us will ever know. **You have to be willing to lay yourself open, and be vulnerable, to be unafraid to take great risk.** In every way, Tiger Woods has the eye of the tiger." Although this is obviously an "athletic" example, think of how these ideas might cross into other areas. Are you willing to be vulnerable and take those risks?

Be ready when opportunity strikes. Opportunities are all over the place. Look for them, create them, and when the time is right, go for it. I never thought I'd write a book. But it wasn't the right time. Suddenly, the idea came, the inspiration hit, I knew it was right, and I was off and running. I'm sure you have lots of ideas about what you could do. Store those things away and when the time is right, make the move: ACT ON YOUR INSPIRATIONS! Trust your instincts. Sure, it needs to be well thought out, the right thing, and realistic, but as the saying goes, "you'll never know unless you try." Lloyd Ward, chief executive officer, secretary general of the United States Olympic Committee and keynote speaker at the 2002 NCAA Foundation Leadership conference, said in his address to the student-athletes, "If you can see it in your mind and feel it in your heart, you can do it."

At the same time, I've seen too many student-athletes put all their eggs in one basket. Many athletes have dreams of making it to the professional ranks, but only a VERY SMALL percentage of college student-athletes will ever realize that dream. According to the NFL Player Development Program, less than 1% of college football players will make an NFL roster. Less than 1%! Only 4% played 3 years or more and the average career is 3.5 years. Maybe that's why some call the NFL – NOT FOR LONG! Likewise, according to the NCAA, only 1.3% of collegiate men's basketball players, 1.0% of women's basketball players, 4.1% of men's hockey players, and 10.5% of baseball players make it professionally. It's great to aim high, but you must look realistically at your chances. Understand the odds. Lying to yourself about those chances will cost you monumentally in the long run. You should always be prepared if those dreams do not come true, because even if you do make it, the average career is short-lived. Most professional athletes retire in their twenties. They leave the game at least thirty-five years before retirement age! The question is not *if* you will have to do something after your career, but *when* and *for how long*. What will you be prepared to do? Just like you should have a "Plan B" if your strategy is not working in competition, you should also have a "Plan B" in case your dreams of making it professionally don't work out and/or for a post professional career.

Thomas Edison remarked, "If we did all the things we were capable of doing, we would literally astound ourselves." In your heart of hearts, what do you think you can achieve? What ARE the possibilities? Complete this sentence for any of the five CHAMPS areas: "What if I…" (tried harder in school, got an internship, did community service, assumed a leadership position, etc.) Take a minute and let your mind wander. What would happen, where would you go and what would you do if you were to invest just a little bit more. Know this – you can get it done. Be willing to venture out of your comfort zone, for without a little risk taking there will be few gains. Robert F. Kennedy said, "Only those who dare to fail greatly, can ever achieve greatly." Lose the labels. Sometimes people don't want to change. They'll accept labels. They'll accept limitations. They'll accept other people's expectations. Break out. College is a fresh start for everyone. Every day is a new day. Challenging your assumptions can be beneficial in many ways, as it allows you to realistically think about and plan for your future.

Before we get to the student-athlete quotes, let me share one more quote from President Theodore Roosevelt, in a speech from 1910. I'm sure many of you have heard this quote at one time or another, but I believe it is at the very heart of CHAMPS/Life Skills:

"The credit belongs to the man who is actually in the arena, who strives valiantly, who knows the great enthusiasm, the great devotions, and spends himself in worthy causes. Who, at best, knows the triumph of high achievement, and who, at worst, if he fails, fails while daring greatly, so that his place shall never be with those cold and timid souls who know neither victory or defeat."

Regardless of your beliefs up to this point, do yourself a favor - take a second and consider the possibilities. You just might surprise yourself.

Academics

Use a **planner**

Go to class

Don't procrastinate!

Utilize resources on campus and in athletics

Get help if you need it

Talk to professors

Academics

Top pieces of advice

1. Always go to class.

2. Learn to manage your time.

3. Get to know and communicate with your professors. Go to office hours!

4. Make academics a priority.

5. Study every day.

6. Look at your syllabi and plan ahead of time.

7. Take advantage of tutors, academic advisors/counselors and support services.

8. Don't procrastinate.

9. Get help as SOON as you need it.

10. Form study groups.

11. Explore your options and be open to new ideas/areas of interest.

12. Challenge yourself academically – set academic goals.

13. Work with your advisors; choose classes/professors wisely.

14. Establish good study habits early.

15. Find a mentor; network with faculty.

16. Use little breaks as study time.

17. Learn how to study and what works best for you.

18. Be committed to learning, not just getting a certain grade.

If we had it to do all over again we would have:

1. Gone to class every day.

2. Studied more and focused on GPA.

3. Worked harder in school from the beginning; take freshman year more seriously.

4. Not procrastinated as much. Studied more in advance.

5. Gone to our professor's office hours.

6. Finish assignments early and see tutors to see if I am doing them correctly.

7. Done the extra problems that are "suggested" work.

8. Utilized more of the resources that were available.

9. Gotten more advice on post-college career options.

10. Gotten help as soon as I started to have problems.

11. Worked more closely with on campus advisors.

12. Participated in class more.

General Thoughts

The most important aspect to succeeding academically is attending class. Even when you don't think class is worth attending, you learn a lot of information that is helpful in exams just by being there. - *Tennis*

You KNOW you can produce as an athlete – but many athletes don't even challenge themselves to produce academically. If you can approach your academics with the same determination as you do your athletics, you might be surprised at what you can accomplish. - *Track and Field*

Although the freshman year is a transitional year, make the most of it. Focus on school your freshman year. Your freshman year grades count, and they will later help you, or hurt you. I thought it didn't matter until my major classes began, and later found out it does play a part. - *Softball*

Be honest with yourself about the environment that you put yourself in and see if it is the most conducive to doing well academically. Make sure that you spend some time with others who are motivated to do well in school. - *Golf*

If you find you are struggling in a class GET HELP. There is nothing wrong with asking for help and the sooner you do, the sooner you'll get back on track. - *Soccer*

Take a look at your syllabus and mark every important date on your calendar. Also, make sure you get all the points you can by doing the little things. Teachers like to see you putting in the extra effort. - *Softball*

Really plan your time – think ahead to how tired you will be after practice/game and do your work before. – *Field Hockey*

Get sleep. I know that hanging out until 4 am is a blast but it truly disrupts one's ability to focus in the classroom and on the court. Everyone is going to do it here and there but try and be responsible about it. - *Volleyball*

When it's all over, you don't want to look back and say, "Shoot – if only I would have tried more in this class I could have had such a better grade." Push yourself. It really does not cut into your social time that much. – *Golf*

Take one class that you would have never taken. – *Soccer*

Who is the person that chooses the textbooks, the material to be covered, when the tests are, the questions on the test, and how the tests are graded? The Professor, so don't you think that it's a good idea to get to know him or her? - *Softball*

Schedule some days with late classes (or none) to catch up on homework or sleep. – *Cross Country/Track and Field*

See teachers BEFORE tests to see if you're on the right track. They'll help you in what to study for! - *Gymnastics*

Know your study techniques, what works best for you. Also, cramming will/could get you the grade, but then why are you studying? - *Swimming*

When the situation seems impossible, envision your goal and remember that what you are doing is helping to accomplish that goal. (Even if it's a dumb class and you can't see the worth in it). – *Volleyball/Softball*

Use summer school as a tool to get ahead. – *Basketball*

Go to all class lectures because you will miss a lot for away games. And make sure you talk to your advisor to get the best teachers. - *Soccer*

There is always enough time as long as you make it. Study during breaks between classes; take your books with you on road trips. Do homework whenever you have even a little time. Maybe it will cut into your sleep sometimes, but don't tell me you don't have enough time. - *Football*

Talk to advisors – both in academics and your major about a 4-year plan. Don't take an easier class because it fits better; take what you need in order to accomplish your goals. – *Swimming*

It's much more difficult to raise your GPA after a rough start than to maintain a good GPA throughout. – *Track and Field*

Get work done on the bus/van. You'll waste a lot of precious time traveling! – *Soccer*

Help others because explaining to someone else only solidifies things more in your own mind. – *Basketball*

Take notes on everything so you can look at it later. Classes are not every day so you will forget, even if you think you knew it. - *Volleyball*

Prioritize! Not just school, sports and social life, but also prioritize your classes. Find out which ones need more time than others. – *Football*

Make sure YOU know exactly what courses you need to graduate – advisors are great but everyone can make mistakes. – *Golf*

Take heavier loads during the first two years of college when only completing general education classes such that when you reach your major courses you can take a lighter load. Depending on your major, school may only get more difficult and it will be nice to be able to focus on your harder courses. - *Track and Field*

Challenging yourself by taking harder classes feels good – you are testing your limits mentally also. – *Swimming*

Study every day. If you start early you will not be so overwhelmed. Use note cards – they really work! – *Volleyball*

Get to know your teachers – sit in the front row, ask questions, have a dialogue in class, make eye contact, go to office hours. In short, be visible to your teacher. He/she will remember you when they have to grade your papers and tests. Also, go to class. It's only half as much time as you had to do in high school. You learn just by being there. - *Football*

Take school seriously because the better you perform in the classroom, the easier it is to perform well in your sport. – *Golf*

Study to comprehend the material, not to memorize it. Try to apply the material you are studying in real life situations. – *Track and Field*

Answer the questions in class when given the opportunity. You WILL remember the correct answer, if you were correct or incorrect (plus it shows you are paying attention). – *Swimming*

Go to any study groups that are available. – *Volleyball*

Don't be fooled into thinking college is easy due to an easy freshman year. - *Wrestling*

It's more about diligence than intelligence. – *Track and Field*

Get paper drafts done early and have TAs or professors read them. – *Volleyball*

Build a relationship with your professor so that you become a person and not just another name or number. - *Football*

Don't always wear your athletics clothes to school because the professor should see that you are not only an athlete but a serious student as well. - *Diving*

Get numbers and e-mails of people from your classes so that if you ever need help then you can call or e-mail them. - *Soccer*

EAT HEALTHY! If you don't, by the end of the year your body will be dead, plus I felt I studied better and could do more work when I had fruit instead of cookies or chocolate. – *Baseball*

Form study groups/study buddies – these really help! – *Track and Field/Cross Country*

Rewrite your notes to help you study for a test. Do it when you are actually studying and not just to make them neater after class.

This way, you just went to that day of class all over again and right before the test. - *Volleyball*

When you have to miss class, get notes from more than 1 person and get them from someone who's doing WELL in the class! - *Gymnastics*

Work closely with advisors and be knowledgeable about your path to graduation. Find a professor in your field of study/career choice to serve as a mentor. – *Football*

Listen – don't just hear what your professors are saying, really LISTEN. – *Baseball*

Challenge yourself academically. Don't be afraid of stereotypical norms related to the subject matter (i.e. girls shouldn't go into math or science.) Don't be intimidated by others' opinion of the class or your insecurity in the field. Be confident in your ability to understand. – *Swimming*

Be committed to learning and not as concerned with grades. – *Lacrosse*

Don't think you can goof off the first year and then try and make up for it later. Even though you can bring it up, the first year affects your GPA. – *Volleyball*

Ask questions of your professors; challenge them and make class interesting and stimulating. Don't be afraid! - *Track and Field*

Sit in the front of the class. I felt kinda stupid at first, but I got more out of it and it's true that teachers will notice. - *Tennis*

On road trips don't sleep on breaks from practice or games while at the hotel and tell yourself you will study later in the night. You will NOT want to pick up a book after a match (or game) or before bed. Do it as early in the day as possible. Plus, when on the bus traveling to the gym, take your notes with you and look over them then too – that can be a good 20 minutes! – *Volleyball*

Pursue an area that interests you even if it is a little more difficult. There is no point in you getting a degree if it is something you wouldn't want to use. If a certain field is hard but interesting, it will still be more enjoyable than classes that are a breeze but absolutely boring. – *Track and Field*

Take subjects that are interesting to you (or even something you know little about) so you can apply what you learn in day-to-day experiences. I took a class in women's studies that completely changed how I looked at things. – *Swimming*

It's not necessarily how "smart" you are – you just have to know *what* to study and *how* to study. When you can just focus on the important stuff, it saves time! – *Tennis*

As Division 1 athletes, it's very easy for us to pour all of our efforts into competition and to put school on the sidelines. We do this because we see the benefits of our work in improved performance, but we don't feel there are equal rewards to putting the same effort into our schoolwork. I guarantee those benefits will be realized when the competition is over. – *Golf*

Don't talk to professors about missing class or tests in front of other students. Go to their office hours if you can. –*Baseball*

Be persistent – never quit. No matter how hard the assignment may be, keep trying. You won't get anywhere if you just give up. – *Volleyball*

College is nothing like high school. Your teachers will not baby you. – *Swimming*

Academics is a game. Play the game by talking to people about what classes they've taken, and who taught them. This way you can avoid the bad classes and teachers and at the same time get the opportunity to learn from inspirational teachers. – *Track and Field*

It is often easy to simply spend most of our time in the athletic community. But it is immeasurably important for the student-athlete to get involved with the academic community. – *Football*

When all is said and done, and it's time for you to leave the school you are attending, look back and ask yourself, "Has this place left a mark on me, and most importantly, have I left a mark on this place?" Leave your mark, and make it a good one. - *Basketball*

Make sure you're on time to class (they notice when you're late) and stay til the end. That's when they give assignments or important announcements are made. – *Gymnastics*

Always know that you can succeed if you're just willing to try. Lots of people resign themselves to being B or C students when there is greater potential there. – *Track and Field*

Stick post-it notes of information you need to learn and know all over the house – especially on the fridge! This way you see them all the time and they will be on your mind and easier to remember. - *Volleyball*

Ask to do extra credit if you're doing bad in a class - *Baseball*

Everybody is intelligent; it's a matter of recognizing your potential and passion and pursuing it. Academic results and grades are subjected to the level of interest you show in the material. - *Swimming*

Don't be afraid to ask for help. Even the most unapproachable teachers are willing to sit down with you and go over the material. – *Crew*

The key to success is to budget time properly. Get to know yourself. Understand what it is going to take for you to succeed and adapt to that reality. Not all students need to study for 8 hours a night. And not all students can get by with a relatively small amount of studying. Know your needs and budget time accordingly. Academic success is dependent on priorities. – *Football*

Make sure you understand the problems in the book and the ones given in class and ask help of classmates and TAs. I was afraid at first to seem ignorant of everything when I asked dumb questions but they really helped me. I made note cards of everything in my notes and went through the information until I could recall what was written on them without look at the backs. – *Track and Field*

Get your homework and papers done before they are due because there will be times when something comes up or you'll want to go out – plus you can never count on how much energy you'll have after practice. – *Baseball*

The more you challenge yourself academically, the better your time management will be. Having good time management will then trickle into every other aspect of your life. - *Swimming*

Go to all your classes every day. When teachers see you making an effort they are more willing to help you out later. – *Volleyball/Softball*

Participate in class discussions. Ask questions. By speaking up it shows that you care about the material and want to learn. If you can't ask during class, go to your professor during their office hours and ask questions. You will learn the material better if you focus on actively participating in the class. Although the syllabus doesn't always specify the percentage of your grade that depends on participation, it is still crucial to your academic success. – *Crew*

Obstacles overcome and how we did it

Having 4 tests in the same week is awful. To deal with that, I started studying weeks in advance for each test. If you do things little by little, it won't be so bad. – *Volleyball*

My fear of failure. When I was getting ready for college I was so afraid that I was not going to be able to handle it. Besides trying to learn how to live on my own, away from my parents, I had to worry about passing all of my classes; I wanted to please my parents, my coaches, and my teammates. Oh, the stress I felt! I was successful because I got to know my professors, used my tutors and I scheduled my time well. – *Softball*

Procrastination – I would wait until the day before to start studying for a test because it was one of my "easier" classes and I thought in the back of my mind I could get away with it. A test is a test. Even when I studied all night it wouldn't be an "all out effort" and I never felt confident that I knew the material. - *Volleyball*

Certain teachers – learn their (teaching) style and adapt and adjust to their style. – *Basketball*

Scheduling classes for school – many times I had to be very organized and talk to many people in order to take the classes I needed as well as those I was interested in. – *Lacrosse*

Like every athlete, I had to manage my schoolwork and athletics – it is imperative that you are organized and know how to manage your time. – *Soccer*

Overcoming the "fear" to speak English (international student). I just told myself to do it, generated by great support from teammates and coaches. – *Basketball*

Develop communication with coaches to make sure they understand that academics are just as important as sports. – *Soccer*

Making the transition from high school to college and from one area of the country to another. I am lucky to have a few close friends and a great support staff at the university all of whom I can talk to and get advice from whenever something may come up. – *Baseball*

I used to do just enough to get by - now I do enough, and more, and my grades show for it. – *Football*

In the beginning, I was too shy to speak up (in class) until I realized that a lot of times my grades depended on it. Focusing on class participation made me study the material more carefully so I would be prepared for class discussion. - *Crew*

I lost all my financial aid and went to a different school. I just kept a positive attitude and tried to work extra to help my parents out. – *Soccer*

My mind frame changed, and my GPA increased. – *Softball*

Coming into college one of the biggest misconceptions that I had was that tutors were only for students who weren't as intelligent as everyone else. In the three years I have been at the University, I have used at least two tutors during every semester. When I go into an auditorium with 100 students, I feel somewhat overwhelmed. I have a hard time focusing because there is so much going on around me, and I don't sense that connection with my professor. With a tutor I can connect with the person that is teaching the information. I can ask more questions and make personal connections with the information. Tutors are not for unintelligent people – they are for people that are striving for a better education. – *Softball*

Switching majors and being behind. I met with professors and got on track. – *Football*

...being a full time, year-round athlete, and Education major has been difficult. Whether it was practice in the morning and afternoons, class during the day and at night or observing children at nearby schools I was continually busy. It was hard to find quiet time. I always found myself planning my day. If I didn't, I was lost the next day. – *Track and Field/Cross Country*

I really struggled with a professor this past semester. I had to go to a tutor for the first time in my life. It was hard to deal with admitting I needed outside help. But I got it and I got an A in a challenging course. – *Basketball*

I was in a difficult major with long lab hours. I sought help from TAs and studied hard/focused during crunch time. Sometimes I had to sacrifice.... for academic reasons. - *Golf*

I was doing bad in school because of poor attendance. But you also have to have courage to approach your professors to seek help and work hard. – *Football*

Sleeping TOO much! I fixed that by writing notes all over the room to motivate myself to complete assignments. – *Track and Field*

Sometimes professors think you are just an athlete. Prove them wrong; gain their confidence by getting to class, being prepared and communicating with them. – *Volleyball*

I haven't overcome it yet, but in December, I will become the first member of my family to ever graduate from college. I think that's a huge obstacle and now I'm beginning a new cycle for my children to follow. - *Basketball*

Finishing through with classes I hated, and getting a good grade in them. – *Soccer*

Professors being a little tough to convince that a different solution can be found. (Solutions were) often found by simply showing respect and attendance the days I am in class – allows him to see that I'm not trying to get out of anything, simply need to do it at a different time. – *Track and Field/Cross Country*

An entire semester down with surgeries. I worked closely with my professors and made sure that we were on the same page and they knew ahead of time what my circumstances would be. They were very helpful in getting me back on my feet academically that semester. - *Football*

Turn in assignments on time. I got a C in a class I should have gotten a B in, but I turned in 3 assignments late. Look at your syllabus too – the dates and other important info are usually on there. - *Gymnastics*

I am dyslexic and I think I overcame it by determination and to prove everyone wrong who thought college would be too hard. – *Soccer*

I could have avoided all sorts of problems if I had asked more questions of students and mentors. Use the resources. This doesn't just mean computer labs or counselors or tutors. This refers to upperclassmen and friends. People who have already gone through the decision-making process – get the expert advice of the experienced. – *Track and Field*

Never let anyone dictate your life, potential or outcome. Someone said the biggest mistake most people make is not making a choice at all. People in general are afraid of failure. Failure, like beauty, is in the eye of the beholder. What looks like something gone wrong, can be a beautiful lesson in how life works. – *Volleyball/Softball*

Set goals for myself, worked hard to achieve them, and I talked to my academic advisor who was also a mentor to me. – *Baseball*

Conflicts between me and some of my professors pertaining to the time missed in class due to athletic events. The main things I had were patience and the will to go back and talk with them. – *Basketball*

Ethnicity and the stereotype of athletes. I believed in myself and had faith in God. – *Football*

I thought I knew enough to get by and I wasn't reaching my potential because of laziness and avoidance. – *Soccer/Softball*

Best thing I ever did for myself in this area

Kept my focus on my education. It is often difficult for scholarship student-athletes because their athletic ability is helping to pay for their education. So there can be a strain on priorities. But at the beginning of my college career, I showed my coaches and the athletic department, in general, that academics were my number one priority. - *Football*

I got all A's and B's - it showed me how much I can achieve and raised my bar of excellence. – *Track and Field*

Take classes that were interesting to me and take classes that I thought I was not good in. In order to challenge myself and, in

addition, I found I had interest in subjects I never thought I would.
– *Lacrosse*

Getting to know my professors on a personal basis. I stop by
their office to chitchat, get help even if I don't need it, and invite
them to my sporting events. Having a close relationship with
your professors can benefit you in many ways. My teachers are
concerned if I miss a class, and they are more willing to help me
with assignments when I have to miss class. –*Volleyball/Softball*

I was open to all areas and sought advice from various teachers.
– *Alpine Skiing*

**Made the decision to come to (my college). I haven't won a
National Championship yet, but this place has changed me
for life, I have made lifelong friends and that's better than any
championship in my book. - *Basketball***

I tape record review sessions (only one teacher hasn't let me). I
haven't gotten lower than a B in any class. – *Softball*

Learned that no matter what situation I was in, I could always
bounce back through hard work and a little determination.
– *Swimming*

I use 3 x 5 cards for everything: questions I have, brainstorming
ideas, or to memorize things for a test. - *Softball*

**I did not procrastinate. The times when I didn't procrastinate
writing a paper or studying for an exam, I did the best. I saw both
sides of the road here, and my life was far better, and I progressed
far more, in times when I was most organized. – *Football***

Established something similar to a study table for many of the
student-athletes that I associate with. – *Track and Field*

Talked with upperclassmen in my major to find out what professors
are helpful to student-athletes. – *Basketball*

Got off to a good start. Get as much help as you can early on. This
way you can put yourself in a much better position the further you
get along with your college career. It is much more difficult if you
put yourself in the position of having to desperately improve your
grades after only the first or second semester. – *Tennis*

Took harder classes in summer school. By far the best thing I ever
did. – *Tennis*

Found old tests to study from. The professors usually don't change their tests too much and this helped A LOT!! – *Baseball*

Realize that this is for me. The education that I am getting is for me only and by just getting through or not trying was not helping myself. I sometimes forgot that I am here for an education first and then sports. Sports are short-lived where as the rest of my life can be affected negatively or positively by how I do in school now. – *Football*

A group of us found an empty classroom and took turns "teaching" the material. It made it more clear for us and easier to remember for the tests. – *Gymnastics*

I did an independent study where I got credit AND career related experience. An advisor told me about how I could do it. It was great. - *Tennis*

Knowing I have an obligation to myself. Trying to maximize the experience of learning in order to better my opportunities in the future. - *Swimming*

There are a lot of more gifted people that have surrounded me throughout my life. What separates me is my work ethic. – *Baseball*

Kept myself as busy as possible and stayed away from television and play station! – *Track and Field/Cross Country*

Hung in there and stayed disciplined. It gets so hard to pick up a book and get into schoolwork when you are trying to focus for a big match. My mind should be on the game and preparing mentally for it, but if it wasn't for good grades I wouldn't even be able to compete. You just need a good system and then stick with it. - *Volleyball*

Formed study groups so I could study while making friends. - *Golf*

I learned to think on my own. – *Baseball*

Maintained positive relationships with the professors, and athletic department staff I admired the most and tried to adopt their positive traits into my own life. - *Volleyball/Basketball/Soccer*

Took classes that were completely unrelated to my course of study. I took classes in French, dance and humanities that just seemed really interesting although they weren't going to apply to my degree. It breaks up the difficulty of required courses and lets you enjoy classes for what they are. – *Track and Field*

Gave change a chance. – *Track and Field/Cross Country*

Not being satisfied with average effort. If you put a lot in, you get a lot out. – *Basketball*

I wasn't afraid to ask questions because most likely someone else has the same question. - *Tennis*

I raised my English grade from 34 to 81 in 4 weeks of school just by getting to know my professor, seeking help and especially working hard. – *Football*

Always introducing myself to my professors and asking a lot of questions. It was very difficult for me to do this, as I've never been very assertive. But it has proven to the most important way to overcome my fears. – *Softball*

Went to every class. I was 4 points away from an A in Econ at the end of the semester and my teacher wound up giving me an A because he said I had been to every class and actively participated. – *Track and Field*

Assessment

WHERE ARE YOU?
WHERE DO YOU WANT TO GO?
HOW WILL YOU GET THERE?

1. Identify your goals in academics (short term/long term).

2. Are you truly and committed to achieving these goals?

3. Are your daily activities congruent with your goals and values?

4. What skill set is necessary for success in academics and which skills can you improve/develop?

5. Identify the changes, challenges and choices you have had to face in this area.

6. What are your assumptions academically? Are they accurate? What is something you were sure of in academics that you aren't sure of anymore?

7. Identify opportunities and resources (on campus and in the athletics department) in this area.

8. What are things you can/can't control in this area?

9. Who is your circle of influence and support system?

10. How are you contributing to or taking away from your academic accomplishments?

11. When are communication skills important in academics and how would you rate yourself?

12. With which quotes could you relate to the most and why?

13. What strategies are you familiar with for note taking and which do you prefer?

    a. Cornell Method (Divides page into 3 sections and lets you pick a preferred note taking method for one section; one section is for review and the last section is to summarize).

b. Outline (Showing the relationship of various ideas using main topics and subtopics).

c. Paragraph (Summarizing a topic in a paragraph).

d. Mind mapping or concept map (A graphic depiction of the connections between key elements in a complex idea).

14. Are you familiar with the SQ4R method for reading comprehension? (Survey; Question; Read; Recite; Reflect; Review).

15. Do you look for the main points and ideas while reading? Highlight about 10-15% of your text (Only what's truly important. Look at the headings and make them into questions that might be asked on a test).

16. Which is your preferred learning style (visual, auditory, kinesthetic)? See your academic counselor for more information.

17. How comfortable are you approaching a professor? What would you say if you had to ask to miss class or a test for competition?

18. How familiar are you with your library and its resources?

19. Have you *challenged* yourself to achieve and *invested* as much academically as much as athletically? Are you *encouraged* as much to do well academically as you are athletically?

20. Do you prepare for classes like you do for practice (on time, focused, ready to go)?

21. How would you rate your time management skills? Do you use 10-15 minute blocks of time to your advantage?

22. Are you easily distracted? What could you do to reduce or eliminate distractions?

23. Do you study when your mind is fresh? Do you study better in the morning or at night? (Try to study during your peak learning times).

24. Do you study your challenging subjects first?

25. Do you have a quiet and comfortable study space?

26. Are there people in each of your classes with whom you could form a study group?

27. Do you use a planner to organize and to know when important tests, assignments and papers are due?

28. Do you know how to compute your GPA?

29. Do you look at the syllabus for every class? (If you understand the syllabus, you understand the expectations.)

30. Are you listening for clues in class from your professor? What are his/her MAIN points?

31. Do you ask questions on a deeper level to understand on a deeper level?

32. Do you read before, pay attention during, and review after class?

33. Do you always do the extra assignments?

34. Are you aware of academic eligibility requirements for participation, including the new requirements (40/60/80 rule)? Yearly GPA requirements? Credits toward your degree, etc.?

35. Could you GRO (grade replacement option) a class to raise your GPA (especially in your major)? Is taking a class Pass/Fail an option?

36. Does your school offer independent studies where you can get course credit and work with someone to get career related experience as well?

37. Are class notes available for purchase? Do your academic counselors or professors have any old tests on file from which you could study?

38. Are there financial aid opportunities or scholarships (institutional, conference, national) for which you might be eligible?

Check with your CHAMPS coordinator for help or to answer any questions.

P-Factor Analysis

➤ **Personalization**

(Setting academic goals and strategies to achieve them; determining priorities; taking initiative; building an academic support system and positive circle of influence; daily choices; self-responsibility and discipline; courage in defining moments; communication skills. **Examples:** going to class every day; talking to professors and advisors; knowing requirements (for major, degree, eligibility); putting yourself in the right academic environment, reading the syllabus, understanding personal preferences, etc.)

- What can I start doing today in the academic area?
- What can I stop doing?
- What can I continue doing?
- How would I rate myself on a scale of 1-10 in academic personalization? _____
- Who can help me in this area?

➤ **Preparation**

(Developing an academic skill set; preparation (based on priorities) for day-to-day tasks and over time; implementing strategies; time management; organization/planning; attention to detail; going above and beyond; quality study time; gaining experience; developing capacity in physical, emotional, mental and spiritual components. **Examples:** having a 4 (or 5) year academic plan; learning note and test taking and reading strategies and techniques; identifying learning style; studying every day; going to review sessions; knowing when tests, papers and assignments are due; forming study groups; finding a mentor; doing all the assignments and any extra ones; not procrastinating; using little breaks to study, etc.)

- What can I start doing today?
- What can I stop doing?
- What can I continue doing?
- How would I rate myself on a scale of 1-10 in academic preparation? _____
- Who can help me in this area?

➤ **Process**

(Day-to-day actions and behaviors, and over time, in relation to academic goals and congruent with stated values and priorities; being fully engaged; staying focused on present task and relevant cues; practicing skills; looking at "how" you do, what you do; consistency in the fundamental process. **Examples:** study habits; going to class every day; studying when your mind is fresh; studying in a quiet place; eliminating distractions; sitting in the front of the class; reviewing notes; using personal preferences to your advantage, etc.)

- What can I start doing today?
- What can I stop doing?
- What can I continue doing?
- How would I rate myself on a scale of 1-10 in academic process? _____
- Who can help me in this area?

➤ **Problem Solving**

(Analyzing root of problem; asking for help early if you need it; utilizing campus/ICA resources, enlisting help of support system; examining/reassessing your strategies, approach and daily process. Developing and identifying options (Plan B); seeking win-win solutions with respect, cooperation, communication, commitment. **Examples:** getting a tutor; working with counselors/advisors; going to writing/learning center; analyzing exams or papers if you don't do well; seeing professors/TAs in office hours; dealing appropriately with stressors; being open to change, etc.)

- What can I start doing today?
- What can I stop doing?
- What can I continue doing?
- How would I rate myself on a scale of 1-10 in academic problem solving? _____
- Who can help me in this area?

➤ **Persistence**

(Staying committed and focused on goals; being determined; being resilient; working through difficult and challenging times. **Examples:** Continuing to try 100% in all academic pursuits;

continuing to work with professors and advisors to do your best, etc.)

- What can I start doing today?
- What can I stop doing?
- What can I continue doing?
- How would I rate myself on a scale of 1-10 in academic persistence? _____
- Who can help me in this area?

➢ **Perspective**

(Confirming/reassessing assumptions; seeing the big picture; being open to other points of view; looking at frame of reference and interpretation of events; learning from each experience; having a positive attitude. **Examples:** exploring different academic areas and majors; being open to different fields/classes/careers; not worrying about one bad grade, etc.)

- What can I start doing today?
- What can I stop doing?
- What can I continue doing?
- How would I rate myself on a scale of 1-10 in academic perspective? _____
- Who can help me in this area?

➢ **Pause**

(Relaxation; reflection; appreciation. **Examples:** taking the time to understand how academics and education impacts your life; appreciating the opportunity you have to get an education; thinking about what you want to do with your degree, etc.)

- What can I start doing today?
- What can I stop doing?
- What can I continue doing?
- How would I rate myself on a scale of 1-10 in academic pausing? _____
- Who can help me in this area?

OVERALL SCORE FOR ACADEMICS: _____

Make The Commitment To Academics!

Game Plan

Athletics

Give **100%** every day

**Have a life
outside
of your sport**

Show good
sportsmanship

Enjoy it!

Take care of **injuries**

Communicate
with coaches

Be mentally and
physically **prepared**

Athletics

Top pieces of advice

1. Give your all every day.
2. Represent your team and the University well.
3. Take care of your body and injuries.
4. Work out on your own and in the off-season.
5. Set goals and strive to achieve them.
6. Be prepared for practice and competition.
7. Get to know your teammates; be a good teammate.
8. Love your sport – have fun.
9. Be positive.
10. Communicate/have a good relationship with your coach.
11. Follow your dreams.
12. Show sportsmanship in victory and defeat.
13. Practice like you play (i.e. intensity level).
14. Don't take it for granted.
15. If you are injured, stay involved with your team as much as possible.
16. Know your body.

If we had it to do all over again we would have:

1. Worked harder in the off-season.
2. Worked more on our own and set up voluntary sessions.
3. Pushed ourselves harder every day – been more intense at practice.
4. Been more aggressive and confident.

5. Spent more time preventing injuries.

6. Taken time to enjoy it more.

7. Understood how much food (nutrition) and sleep affect practice and performance.

8. Worked harder on the mental game.

General Thoughts

Try to enjoy the moment as long as you can because once it is over, you will only get it back through memories – so make them good ones. – *Football*

It's a lot of hard work and requires perseverance and determination. Be ready to put in the time. – *Lacrosse*

The best players don't get that way without working hard. – *Track and Field*

Celebrate (in your head) every time you win or do something well. We too often forget the good and focus on the bad. You might start to realize that there is ALWAYS more good than bad in things that you do. - *Swimming*

Always go above and beyond to succeed. You will be proud to say you did your best. – *Volleyball*

Positive attitude means everything. No matter what position you are on your team, you can improve by having the right attitude. If you are second string (or in this case second boat), you will get better if you keep trying and thinking positively. You are still an important asset to the team. – *Crew*

Logistics are important – be committed to the minute details. – *Track and Field*

Treat your body right – it's your competitive advantage. – *Football*

Always give 100%. Nothing is guaranteed and every day you have an opportunity to do something special. – *Soccer*

Be a team player all the time. Championships aren't won by one person – it takes many to rise to the top. – *Track and Field*

Don't get too high or too low on yourself. It's a lot of pressure the first year that you are playing a Division 1 sport, and no one is perfect their first year. – *Baseball*

With time, I have learned what I need to do to play well and what I need to stop doing. You learn to become your own best friend. - *Golf*

Dedication – push yourself even when you don't believe you can anymore. You have to visualize the long-term goal and make it a reality, slowly but surely. – *Track and Field*

Don't wait until your senior year to take a role on your team. – *Football*

I do not like shoulda, woulda, coulda's. I live by three precious words – DO YOUR BEST. If I do, then I am comfortable, even if I don't like the outcome. We have to learn to accept the past and learn that some things we cannot change, but we can, however, be better prepared in the future. – *Volleyball/Basketball/Soccer*

Never lose the love of the game – that should be why you're playing and why you endure through the tough times. – *Volleyball*

Focus as much as possible and train hard – 4 years isn't a long time. – *Wrestling*

Be coachable, punctual, responsible, mature…and BUST YOUR ASS every chance you get. – *Football*

If you aren't a team leader, be a team supporter. – *Alpine Skiing*

I wish I had had more respect for my body when it came time for sleeping. My freshman year I was afraid I'd miss something. In fact I did: the chance to perform at my best. – *Tennis*

Heart is the key to any sport. You can have as much talent as Michael Jordan but if you don't play with heart…you can only be as good as one of those guys who claim them could have been the next Jordan. – *Volleyball/Softball*

Sometimes I wake up in the morning and my mind starts running. I think about 2,000 things – my future, my sport, and I think I can't waste one second of my life. I wonder about my career, about what I should do, or if I want to do this the rest of my life. Sometimes I wonder if I do all of these things for others or to prove something.

Eventually I realize that I play for myself because it's what I enjoy and it's made me who I am. – *Golf*

Spend more time doing things to prevent injuries before they occur. Ice-baths are great! Use the resources that are available to you. - *Track and Field*

Don't wear yourself out physically or mentally but definitely do the little extra things that will give you confidence and an edge when the important meets/games come up. - *Diving*

Never be arrogant – be privileged! – *Tennis*

Train hard in the weight room. It can make up for what you may lack in talent. Be patient, and let success come to you. - *Golf*

Show your coach that you are interested in getting better. Work hard, put in the extra work, and they will remember your attitude when game time comes around. - *Football*

Realize that you are given an opportunity. Take pride in what you are doing and remember why you are here. Take advantage of these next years of your life. Thousands of people would love to be in your shoes. - *Gymnastics*

I know you hear coaches say it all the time, but be able to honestly look yourself in the mirror after you play. You will lose more than a game if you don't give everything you have. – *Football*

Constantly set realistic goals and monitor them so that you can keep yourself in the present and not think too far ahead. - *Tennis*

Don't assume you're still the best, because college is a different world. To be successful in college athletics, it's better to be humble because instinctively you'll just work harder. - *Track and Field*

Eat healthy and get lots of sleep – those were the biggest things to having tons of energy. – *Baseball*

Relax and smile when competing. Blood, sweat, tears and emotional stress are for practice, not competition. Besides, if racing is too intense, what makes you happy about your sport? - *Swimming*

Be on time. With Coach, "on time" was 5 minutes early. Actually being on time was LATE! – *Softball*

Be enthusiastic. When you do something, do it whole-heartedly and love it. This quality is very contagious, whether it is being excited about a group project in school and getting everybody else as enthused or putting a smile on your teammates faces at the 6:00am practice – especially at the end of the year. We practice a lot and at the end of the year, moods are harder to control. - *Volleyball*

Know that everyone has limitations but that they also have incredible talents. Be exploitative about your talents and try your hardest. Because then, whether you succeed or fail, you know you've tried your best. – *Track and Field*

Never take for granted what you have because there are so many people who would love to be sitting where we are as student-athletes. People say we should get paid. We are being paid, in full, with a free education, something that's going to reward us for the rest of our lives. Appreciate it. - *Basketball*

Sometimes you have to trade an amazing "social" opportunity for what's really important – school and sports. – *Football*

Be aware of your body, mind and the way you affect your team. Pay attention to what your body is lacking – be it sleep, or food. With your mind, pay attention to your ability to focus, your level of focus. Finally, I think it is really important to be aware of how you affect EACH of your teammates. Are the things you tell your teammates making them better or worse? Do you build their self-esteem? Do you push them to get better? - *Volleyball*

Be patient. No matter how things are going or how bad the results are for the moment, it always turns out for the best. Sometimes, going one step back is going to take you two or three steps forward. Remember that this is a very long race. Your heart and your desire to achieve your dreams are bigger than anything. – *Golf*

You don't have to be a captain to be a leader and you aren't always liked by being a leader. You can be disliked, but still respected. - *Soccer*

Always go to practice with a game plan of what you want to accomplish that day. If you're prepared to practice, you will get more out of the allotted practice time. – *Golf*

Believe in yourself – that is an attitude that gets you places in athletics and can transfer to other areas as well. If I had really pushed myself from the inside, perhaps I could have been a little better. – *Track and Field*

Success in college athletics is about longevity – a lot can happen in 4 or 5 years - don't get too high on success and don't get too down on your struggles. – *Football*

Having a good mental game during bad practices helps develop mental strength for competition. - *Swimming*

Leave your personal life, strife, and battles off the practice and competition fields. Focus your negative energy into positive results in competition. – *Volleyball/Basketball/Soccer*

The sport of rowing carries over into all other areas of life. The discipline and respect I learn at practice have helped me succeed with my schoolwork and internships. – *Crew*

Time goes by fast. Sometimes it seems like the work will never end. But when your career is over you realize how much fun it all was. Take time to reflect on the experience while it is happening. Appreciate the opportunity. Play your sport with the joy of your childhood. – *Football*

Train hard and know your body, listen to your body. Nobody knows your body better than you. Coaches are guides for your success but they don't always know how you are feeling. Communication with a coach can achieve great results. - *Swimming*

Try not to let it rule your life. If I had a bad practice or game my whole day or week was ruined. I would be down in my social life and in academics too. Sports are how people have always defined me and how I test myself too. Have other things in your life – balance is the key. – *Volleyball*

It is always hard to find the right path in life and even harder sometimes to find the courage to pursue it. If you are one of the few people in life that want to do something different and, more important, want to be someone different than the others, then you are ahead of the rest. There is not one single champion that does things the way others do them. Every person has their own way to do things. If you want to be different, you have to act differently and think differently. – *Golf*

Obstacles overcome and how we did it

Our team had lots of negativity and many unhappy people. But many of us chose to stay positive and pretty soon those people who brought our team down left so now we have a solid core of determined athletes who love what they do and are devoted to encouraging each other and working as a team to accomplish goals. – *Volleyball*

An injury – I remained relaxed and…focused on aspects that encompassed my training other than running. – *Track and Field*

I had never been exposed to such high competition. At first I choked on high pressure, but now I thrive on it. – *Swimming*

I overcame a very disappointing sophomore season. I went back, practiced hard and proved to myself that there is never a reason to quit. Improvement is always accompanied by hard work. - *Tennis*

Being a non-recruited walk-on at the start of my career. I started out not really feeling like anyone wanted me. I didn't really feel like part of the team for the first year or so. The way I overcame this was that I worked hard to prove myself. There were many days when I experienced major struggles. It was rarely easy. But it was worth it. I found my niche on the team. I was never really a star on the team but I worked my way onto a leadership position. Eventually, I earned a scholarship. - *Football*

Team conflict – be a family on the field, and stay open to others. – *Track and Field*

Changing coaches – I'm now with my third coach and I've found that it's important to build relationships outside of my sport where I can find support. – *Soccer*

At the end of my sophomore year, I was very down on volleyball and myself. I was a bench player the last 2 years, hardly played and was beginning to think I didn't love the game anymore and may never play in college. That summer I was inspired, found the love and passion for the game once again, decided I didn't want to have any regrets and went back to school and became the top starting middle for my team. – *Volleyball*

Constant sickness and over training – it has been hard but through perseverance and work with my coach, I am surviving. – *Swimming*

I quit this season, but came back to finish the season. I worked inside and realized that I was hurting myself and others. – *Basketball*

I hurt my back junior year. I had to rehab for a year but I am finally back now. What I learned is everyone has a role on the team even if you're not a key player. I focused on motivating my team and getting healthy. – *Volleyball*

Trust what the doctors and trainers tell you. They know best. Being injured was definitely one of the hardest things that I have had to deal with as an athlete, but I know that it was also one of those things that will have a lasting impact on my work ethic. I don't think I have ever worked as hard as I did to get back in my whole life. – *Basketball*

Overcame limited playing time by continual work and persistence. – *Hockey*

Being a walk-on. I learned the ropes as fast as I could through interactions with other teammates and was never ashamed to ask a question. - *Track and Field*

I have been out for an entire year, due to three consecutive knee surgeries and my confidence, ability and athleticism suffered, but I continue to try to be a leader and a part of my team. – *Volleyball*

Persevered when times were hard by continuing to always work hard and be positive. Others will be able to look to you as an example and individuals as well as the team are affected positively. – *Football*

In being the team captain my obstacle was always being the middleman between the coach and the team. This was hard since I am not good with conflict. It is so hard for me not to say to people what will make them happy and what they want to hear, but I just had to do my job and hoped people understood. Strong will and trust are very important. – *Volleyball*

Getting adjusted to a more intense lifestyle. I was scared and had little support on campus. So I quit my first fall season. But when I did a "self-inventory" I realized how large a part of my life being an athlete is, and I came back. – *Field Hockey*

Changing my style of play to fit the team. – *Soccer*

I was the only ethnic basketball player and for me that was an obstacle. With the help from my friends and teammates, it was easily overcome. – *Basketball*

Maintaining a positive attitude when I practice. My worst practice had the most mental significance of how I performed. Now, in every situation I look for the good and celebrate, no matter how small. - *Swimming*

When I first got to the United States (international student), it was very hard to accept my differences and weaknesses, and more than once I was afraid to ask for help. The best thing by far, that any student-athlete can do is to have good communication with your coach and teammates. It is a lot easier to achieve your dreams being close with the people that you spend your time with. – *Golf*

I let other problems in my life come into practices, but learned to separate the two. – *Volleyball*

Trying to get along with different personalities on the team and dealing with negative people. I didn't let them get to me and I tried to be an example for them. – *Crew*

When I was sad or homesick or just down after a bad day, it always made me feel better to write down my feelings in a journal. I could express all my feelings without having to listen to others' opinions, and wanted to make sure my heart did not become hard. It was the only way I felt together and found peace within me. – *Golf*

The only obstacle I struggled with was my weight. My coach and I had different views on my weight. By my junior year, I stopped struggling with my weight and just did the best I could. – *Volleyball/ Basketball/Soccer*

The pressure of being voted team captain as a sophomore – I had to learn quickly how to gain respect. I did this by giving my teammates respect. – *Baseball*

I've gone through 4 knee surgeries. Doctors told me that my basketball career was over and that I'd never be able to do the things I once did. I'm beginning my third season of playing the sport I love since then. The knee injuries, though painful, I can't say I would change – they have made me a stronger person. – *Basketball*

My coach and I clashed for some reason. It took a serious disagreement for both of us to realize how much we weren't getting anywhere and how much our "attitudes" with each other were affecting the unity of the team. The team captains decided to call a captain's meeting to address our problems with our coach, which we invited him to attend. We voiced our concerns and gripes, he voiced his. We cleared all the tension and moved on to have a good season. – *Volleyball/Softball*

I was injured and out for a year. I got involved in other things – community service and an association/organization in my field (marketing). It took my mind off my injury and helped me feel more productive than just sitting around and rehabbing. – *Gymnastics*

A mental obstacle of being THE guy. I think it mostly took time, but talking to the coaches about it and preparing myself mentally-knowing my opponent's strengths and weaknesses - really helped. I just tried to have confidence in my abilities. – *Baseball*

I had to prove myself to the team and the coaches since I was basically a walk-on. I was absolutely frustrated in the beginning and felt like a big nothing and a waste since they wouldn't even let me compete in away meets for the team. I decided that I needed to be happy with being an athlete and just do it for the pure enjoyment of it, not what anyone else thought of my performances. That really helped - *Track and Field*

The main thing that got me through my injuries (broken foot and dislocated shoulder) was believing in myself – knowing I could do it and staying positive kept my inner fire lit; it kept that drive to become a better athlete alive inside me. Also, knowing that I would be a stronger person as a result of my trials only made me better off in the end. - *Diving*

Best thing I ever did for myself in this area

I realize that the things I learn from the sport will be essential in other areas. The communication skills make me more effective when interacting with teachers or managers. The team and personal goal setting allows me to achieve objectives that I set for myself in all other areas. The process of being a successful student-athlete is the same process of being successful in life. - *Crew*

Made the most out of every experience, every thing and every person that came my way. I can honestly look back and say I have no regrets and feel great about it. – *Volleyball/Basketball/Soccer*

Dedicated myself to this sport because I love it - working hard in the weight room, eating healthy and preparing mentally. There is nothing better than playing for a great university, being recognized for what I do and appreciated for that. – *Baseball*

Understand that it was a team sport. It wasn't about the personal accolades or about my playing time. Although I would have loved to play more, I think it helped me keep the proper perspective about the team. While I contributed on the field, the smartest thing that I did was to find other ways to help out the team. Whether this was helping out younger players or serving as a leader on the team, I always tried to make myself valuable to the success of our team. - *Football*

I let the pressure make me work harder. We have a competitive team and I wanted to be the best I could be. Everyone wants to be in the top boat. Rather than worrying too much about my rank on the team, I put my energy into staying dedicated and learning as much as I could to improve. In the end, I was right where I wanted to be. – *Crew*

Choosing to attend a Historically Black College and participate in a sport that not a lot of African Americans are involved in. – *Swimming*

Realized that my sport is just a game, not my entire life. – *Softball*

I realized that there would be great moments as well as frustrating ones throughout my college career. Understanding this allowed me to positively handle the good moments and, more importantly, gave me the ability to bounce back when the disappointments were upon me. - *Tennis*

I was always willing to keep trying. That's the only reason I can find for how I succeeded. – *Track and Field*

Stepping up and being a leader as a sophomore. – *Soccer*

Took many hours of my own extra time to work harder and learn the game. – *Volleyball*

Challenged the process. – *Track and Field*

Not to give in and never be satisfied with where I was. At one point, I also had to make a choice of which sport to play. I decided to walk on for football. I look back on all the pain (of injuries) and struggles that I went through and know it will always be worth it. - *Football*

As a freshman, I showed everyone I was there to play and wasn't scared about pushing myself and showing people what I'm made of. – *Basketball*

Started to watch what foods I was eating. When I started eating the right foods my whole body felt different and I was able to perform better. – *Track and Field*

Became more positive. I was very negative and getting down on myself wasn't helping myself or my team. There are very few days that you will be at your 100%, absolute best - for whatever reason. Now on days I'm maybe not playing as well in one area, I still try to COMPETE as hard as I can and help my team in other ways. I can take pride in knowing I gave my best effort on that day. - *Baseball*

Sports have taught me to accept me for who I am. I realized it is through my hard work and diligence and the support and resources of others that I got to where I am. I know that where I go depends on my attitudes, perceptions, and pride. – *Track and Field/Cross Country*

Assessment

WHERE ARE YOU?
WHERE DO YOU WANT TO GO?
HOW WILL YOU GET THERE?

1. Identify your goals in athletics (short term/long term).

2. Are you truly committed to achieving these goals?

3. Are your daily activities congruent with your goals and values?

4. What skill set is necessary for success in your sport and which can you improve/develop?

5. Identify the changes, challenges and choices you have had to face in athletics.

6. What are your assumptions athletically? Are they accurate? What is something you were sure of in athletics that you aren't sure of anymore?

7. Identify opportunities and resources (on campus and in the athletics department) in this area?

8. What are things you can/can't control in this area?

9. Who is your circle of influence and support system?

10. How are you contributing to or taking away from your athletic accomplishments? From your team at practice every day?

11. When are communication skills important in athletics and how would you rate yourself?

12. With which quotes could you relate to the most and why?

13. Rate yourself overall in the dimensions of the physical, emotional, mental and spiritual aspects of your sport? Rate your capacity in each of those areas? What about the technical and strategic components? (For more information on the mental game, also see peak performance consultant Jeff Janssen's website at www.jeffjanssen.com).

14. Are you a good teammate? In what ways do you support your teammates and coaches? What is your role on your team?

15. How would you rate your work ethic? Do you give 100% every day?

16. Rate yourself, in general, in terms of quality of practice vs. quantity?

17. Are you aware of the role periodization plays in peak performance? Check with your strength and conditioning coach for more information.

18. Identify situations in your sport when your focus needs to be more broad or narrow? Internal or external?

19. How fierce a competitor are you? When winning? When losing?

20. Are you afraid of failure? Success? How does this affect you or the approach to your sport?

21. How do you deal with the stress of being a student-athlete? What are your biggest stressors?

22. Do you try to prevent injuries and/or take care of injuries immediately?

23. Do you do what your coaches and trainers ask of you on a daily basis?

24. Do you practice like you compete?

25. Do you prepare for every competition the same way, regardless of your opponent? What routines and mindset do you need to have to be at your best?

26. Are you humble in victory and gracious in defeat?

27. Do you take something positive away from every experience?

28. Describe your off season habits?

29. Would you say you have a good balance in your life? How does being involved in other things affect your athletics?

30. Do you think student-athletes should be paid? Why or why not?

31. How much is a scholarship worth at your university? (Including tuition, books, dorms, travel, equipment, meals, medical services, etc.)

32. If you ever are interested in agents, are you aware of individuals, or organizations that can advise and help you? (Coaches, compliance office, professional sports counseling panels, NCAA, professional associations, etc.)?

P-Factor Analysis

➤ **Personalization**

(Setting athletic goals and strategies to achieve them; determining priorities; taking initiative; building an athletic support system and positive circle of influence; daily choices; self-responsibility and discipline; courage in defining moments; communication skills. **Examples:** giving 100% every day; listening to your coach; being a good teammate; showing good sportsmanship, etc.)

- What can I start doing today in the academic area?
- What can I stop doing?
- What can I continue doing?
- How would I rate myself on a scale of 1-10 in athletic personalization? _____
- Who can help me in this area?

➤ **Preparation**

(Developing an athletic skill set (physical and mental); preparation (based on priorities) for day-to-day tasks and over time; implementing strategies; time management; organization/planning; attention to detail; going above and beyond; quality practices; gaining experience; developing capacity in physical, emotional, mental and spiritual components. **Examples:** getting extra help, doing extra training; taking care of your body; getting enough sleep; injury prevention; working out in the off season; being at your best every day at practice; practicing like you play; being a student of the game, etc.)

- What can I start doing today?
- What can I stop doing?
- What can I continue doing?

- How would I rate myself on a scale of 1-10 in athletic preparation? _____
- Who can help me in this area?

> **Process**

(Day-to-day actions and behaviors, and over time, in relation to athletic goals and congruent with stated values and priorities; being fully engaged; staying focused on present task and relevant cues; practicing skills; looking at "how" you do what you do; consistency in the fundamental process. **Examples:** practice habits; doing the little things on and off the field on a daily basis to make you better; practicing skills daily, getting the most out of practice, videotaping practice or competition, etc.)

- What can I start doing today?
- What can I stop doing?
- What can I continue doing?
- How would I rate myself on a scale of 1-10 in athletic process? _____
- Who can help me in this area?

> **Problem Solving**

(Analyzing root of problem; asking for help early if you need it; utilizing campus/ ICA resources, enlisting help of support system; examining/reassessing your strategies, approach and daily process; developing and identifying options (Plan B); seeking win-win solutions with respect, cooperation, communication, commitment. **Examples:** analyzing physical, mental, emotional, spiritual, technical, and strategic components of daily practice/competitions; communicating/working with coaches, dealing with stress, versatility, etc.)

- What can I start doing today?
- What can I stop doing?
- What can I continue doing?
- How would I rate myself on a scale of 1-10 in athletic problem solving? _____
- Who can help me in this area?

> **Persistence**

(Staying committed and focused on goals; being determined; being resilient; working through difficult and challenging times;

<u>Examples:</u> continue trying your hardest; continue working with coaches and trainers to be your best, remaining dedicated, etc.)

- What can I start doing today?
- What can I stop doing?
- What can I continue doing?
- How would I rate myself on a scale of 1-10 in athletic persistence? _____
- Who can help me in this area?

➤ **Perspective**

(Confirming/reassessing assumptions; seeing the big picture; being open to other points of view; looking at frame of reference and interpretation of events; learning from each experience; having a positive attitude. <u>Examples:</u> not getting too excited with wins or too disappointed with losses; having friends and activities outside of athletics; appreciating what athletics gives you/teaches you, etc.)

- What can I start doing today?
- What can I stop doing?
- What can I continue doing?
- How would I rate myself on a scale of 1-10 in athletic perspective? _____
- Who can help me in this area?

➤ **Pause**

(Relaxation; reflection; appreciation. <u>Examples:</u> giving your body and mind enough recovery time; thinking about what role athletics plays in your life; relating lessons learned in athletics to other life skills, etc.)

- What can I start doing today?
- What can I stop doing?
- What can I continue doing?
- How would I rate myself on a scale of 1-10 in athletic pausing? _____
- Who can help me in this area?

OVERALL SCORE FOR ATHLETICS: _____

Make The Commitment To Athletics!

Game Plan

Personal Development

Develop
communication skills

Eat right

Stay **true to yourself**

Manage your money

Get enough sleep!

Get involved with
leadership groups

Have balance
in your life

Personal Development

1. **Health and Wellness**

   (*Nutrition, drugs/alcohol, sexual responsibility, hazing, gambling, etc.*)

2. **Leadership and Character**

   (*Citizenship, decision-making, ethics, sportsmanship, diversity, personal accountability, etc.*)

3. **Essential Life Skills**

   (*Time/stress management, financial responsibility, manners/etiquette, communication skills, etc.*)

Top pieces of advice

1. Manage your time.

2. Be responsible in all areas.

3. Eat the right foods to keep you training and performing at your best.

4. Get involved in leadership boards and activities.

5. Be a leader in your own way.

6. Make sure you get enough sleep.

7. Stay true to yourself; be your own person.

8. Have a life and friends outside of sports.

9. Find a good balance in all areas.

10. Set goals, prioritize, and plan.

11. Surround yourself with the right people.

12. Develop your communication skills.

13. Understand money matters.

14. Control the things you can, and don't stress out over things you can't.

If we had it to do all over again we would have:

1. Made an effort to meet more people.

2. Not been afraid to ask questions.

3. Socialized with others, not just student-athletes.

4. Gotten involved in activities outside of athletics.

5. Learned to balance school, athletics and social life better.

6. Been more organized.

7. Gotten more sleep.

8. Challenged myself more to go out of my comfort zone.

9. Learned how to manage my money better.

10. Developed my skills as a leader.

11. Believed in myself more.

12. Learned more about nutrition and supplements.

13. Communicated better when faced with some of the new and difficult decisions that come with college life.

14. Learned to manage my stress better.

General Thoughts

Understand that you are a part of something bigger than yourself.
– *Football*

Be interested in what other people are doing/striving for. They will appreciate that you are making an effort to hear about their lives. Carrying on a genuine conversation is much cooler than trying to fit in. – *Diving*

Leaders are born unexpectedly. In situations where no one wants to take charge or take the blame, leaders emerge to take the extra burden. But once you become a leader there is no turning back. People will depend and lean on you from that moment forward. – *Volleyball/Softball*

In order to meet people, it's necessary to get out there and be seen. Community service, leadership groups, etc., are great ways to meet other student-athletes. – *Golf*

Surround yourself with friends that will help you make positive decisions. – *Volleyball/Basketball/Soccer*

Just be yourself, be safe and don't go anywhere alone! Have fun and take it slow, because when you are done with athletics, and even school, you are going to want it all back…I do! - *Gymnastics*

Get involved early, and don't take anything in life so seriously that you lose sight of the big picture. Have fun at whatever you do. This includes your sport…. - *Golf*

Be open to the world. This is a big place, an environment where you have to learn how to live your own life. At the same time, you have to learn how to live with other people and cooperate with them, because you cannot succeed on your own. Also, learn how to listen, learn how to learn. Trust the people who are here to help you. Remember, that if you have a problem, what they tell you and what they advise you, is part of the solution. - *Track and Field*

I never really paid attention to how much sleep I got or what kinds of foods I put in my body before college. I have learned that my body is really a fine-tuned machine and I can maximize my abilities by taking a couple minutes each day to plan out what I will eat. The worst thing to do is to come home from practice and be so ravenous that you just eat the first thing you see! - *Diving*

Don't get sucked into doing things you don't want to do – try to stay true to yourself. At the same time, don't shun people who do things you don't necessarily agree with. Rather, take people for who they are and learn from them. - *Tennis*

Never assume. Most people know the saying and it's true. Some of the most helpful people are those you would have never thought to ask. – *Volleyball/Softball*

Watch what you buy in the store (and question is this good for me?) – *Track and Field*

Show an interest in your roommate's daily activities. Know their interests so you can respect them for who they are. A roommate can be your best available friend in a time of need. - *Swimming*

Participation in SAAC, in some capacity, is something I would, and do, recommend for every student-athlete. The benefits of this experience cannot be overestimated. - *Football*

Keep some time for yourself, to be alone, to relax or to just have fun. - *Tennis*

Don't let anyone else dictate who you are and what your values and morals "should" be. - *Volleyball*

Get involved in something that has nothing to do with athletics and make friends there. It is very refreshing to be around people who don't have athletics to worry about and who socialize with you on another level. – *Golf*

Be determined to make some kind of impact – decide what that is and go after it whole-heartedly. – *Volleyball*

Remember that no matter where you go, someone will probably recognize you. Before you do something stupid or say something you might regret, remember you represent your university and the athletic department. - *Track and Field*

Define a good leader to yourself and then pursue those attributes. - *Swimming*

The most important thing is to find BALANCE in your life. Be careful to not lose the real you. We choose this life but what I'm trying to say is you need family, friends and a life outside of sports. – *Golf*

Take care of priorities – not needs and wants. – *Basketball*

If you take supplements, make sure you know what you are taking. Don't just take a random thing because some muscle-head told you that it will make you better. Do research. Never put anything in your body that you aren't sure of. - *Baseball*

Make sure you are involved in other things besides athletics. Don't let sports define all that you are. – *Volleyball*

We think it is always hard to find someone in life that will understand us, and support us, but if you look around, there are people just like you that feel the same way. We all need something from others and we can all give something to others. This is what makes people special. – *Golf*

Remember people's names. You can't comprehend the respect you can earn. – *Swimming*

Lead by example – people may doubt what you say but they will always believe what you do. – *Football*

Try not to call home too much at the beginning because you will get too homesick. Use the time at the beginning to build friendships with others because that's the time when you build the strongest bonds. – *Diving*

Get involved in everything you can. Make contacts with everyone you meet. It is a privilege to be an athlete. Athletes are an elite group of people who will change the world. – *Volleyball*

Don't accept hazing from anyone. No one is allowed to force you to do anything. – *Tennis*

There are always ways to become a better person, change any program and make something right. Go the distance. – *Volleyball*

Don't trust everyone you meet. – *Diving*

Have no regrets; make yourself happy, not others; do all that you can while you are young and have the opportunities to lead that many students never get a chance to do. – *Track and Field*

Time management can make your life so much easier. Good time management = good grades = happy athletes. – *Soccer*

Deal with anger by using your mind and your words. You are more likely to change someone with your words rather than your fists. Just because you might be bigger or stronger, that doesn't solve the problem. Walk away if you have to. Anger is all about control - you must learn to control it within yourself or someone else will do it for you. - *Football*

Self-discipline is the foundation for health and happiness. - *Track and Field*

Treat your body like you want to be here awhile. – *Baseball*

Be responsible in every area – financial, academics, athletics, and social (dating, friends and family). – *Track and Field*

Live on campus for a couple years. Dorm life, or on campus living, helps you meet people and keeps you focused on what you are in college for. – *Basketball*

Stay healthy – eat right – if not for yourself, for the ones who love you. – *Swimming*

Accept each challenge as a stepping-stone in your life and allow it to shape you into who you will become. – *Ice Hockey*

Monitor the money you spend on the weekends! – *Basketball*

If you work hard toward a goal that you really want to accomplish that determination will most likely be contagious and inspire others. How can you resist the opportunity for success? – *Track and Field/Cross Country*

Be ready to encounter anything. – *Cross Country*

Be careful with money. I am pretty good with money – if I have extra, it will burn a hole in my pocket quick, and if I don't I can go a very long time being stingy if necessary. However, I am always hearing stories about other athletes who get into credit card messes and such – be disciplined. – *Volleyball*

Give a compliment to someone at least once a day (you never know when you might need one.) – *Swimming*

Living in a dorm makes you a better person. You are stuck in a confined space with another person, usually not like you, and forced to get to know them and get along with them, much like one will have to do in the real world. – *Baseball*

Always talking is less effective. Listen more, speak less and your words will be more powerful. – *Softball*

Communication skills are vital and a building block for everything else. – *Volleyball*

I didn't get involved (in leadership groups) until my sophomore year because I didn't know about the opportunities. Now, at the end of my junior year I want to be more involved in all sorts of groups and boards. Find out what you can be in and be in it. - *Swimming*

Even if you don't agree with a person, or even like them, give them the respect that they deserve. - *Volleyball/Softball*

I've learned that there are different kinds of leaders. I always thought leaders were the best players or most vocal ones. Now I know you can be a leader in lots of different ways. – *Tennis*

Learn how to say one simple word: NO. It can make your life much easier. – *Field Hockey*

Don't have sex just because you can. – *Football*

Learn to embrace adversity – it only makes you stronger and develops your character. – *Volleyball*

It's better to live on campus and get to know your teammates better. We eat dinner together and can visit one another. People who have lived off campus always seem more isolated. - *Crew*

Ignorance is bliss and knowledge is priceless...choose wisely. – *Wrestling*

Supplements – be aware of what you are taking and if they have any banned substances – they don't list everything that is in these supplements. – *Baseball*

Make friends in class even if it's one per class – you'll be surprised how much you might have in common. Also, keep your word (promise) if you say you will. - *Swimming*

Seek knowledge and be open to the wisdom of others. – *Football*

Communicate directly with people if you have a problem; talk about it, don't whine. – *Volleyball*

Eat good food all day long and you'll be surprised at the difference at practice. – *Diving*

Become a leader in your own fashion – through empathy, example and excellence. – *Ice Hockey*

America has a culture that is not found anywhere else on earth. It will initially take some time to become acclimated, but eventually you will find that there are many riches here that you won't find anywhere else. The main thing is to give it time. – *Tennis*

Make a difference in your life by asking questions about issues that make you wonder. - *Track and Field*

Find an outlet away from school and athletics in order to keep your sanity. – *Golf*

I have always been crazy about my weight. It ruled my life. The first thought in my mind every day when I woke up was how unhappy I was with my body. So my freshman year I became anorexic and lost a lot of weight. But I learned to be healthy and not stress about weight. It was hard at first to think this way but... you have an obligation to your team, your school and yourself to be in top shape. - *Volleyball*

De-stress whenever possible (even if you aren't very stressed!). - *Track and Field*

Don't compare yourself to others. If we were all meant to be carbon copies of each other, life would be boring. Comparing yourself to others is self-destructive. – Softball

Remember that you are always in uniform. If you do something that you shouldn't, it gives a bad reputation to your whole team, and that's not fair to your teammates. Think about the consequences and who all might be affected. - Tennis

Take whatever opportunities are available because more times than not, opportunities are once in a lifetime. - *Track and Field*

Choose wisely when picking roommates. They can make your life miserable if you can't get along, or if they do not have respect for your needs. – *Football*

Communication is the key to success – in the classroom, on the court, and in life. – *Basketball*

Take care of yourself, then others. Get sleep, eat right, etc. – and then worry about people around you. – *Ice Hockey/Tennis*

I am learning that making money isn't always about how much I can make to go on a shopping spree for the newest fashions. There are far more important things in life like dental insurance, health insurance, car payments, life insurance and for that air conditioner that just went out and now you have to spend a ton of money to fix it. – *Volleyball*

Try and keep your life balanced. I loved sports but if they became everything to me then they became stressful. The same is true of academics and extracurricular activities. - *Track and Field*

Eat 3 meals a day – especially breakfast – it makes you feel more alert for your morning classes. - *Baseball*

Take leadership roles even if you don't feel quite ready. It'll help – I promise! – *Track and Field/Cross Country*

Treat others with respect. Recognize their boundaries and needs. – *Tennis*

The worst thing to do is not communicate. If there is an issue or you don't know what to do from a certain point, voice your concerns, talk to someone who may be able to help you. Find alternate solutions but most importantly, don't give up. – *Volleyball/Softball*

Speak up and never give up if you find something that needs to be changed. – *Cross Country*

Keep yourself healthy. Life in school and athletics is stressful and there are certain ways that every person finds to relieve that stress. Don't do things that are ultimately going to create more problems. – *Track and Field*

Always keep in mind that someone is out there to help you if you ever have a problem. You just have to know who to ask. – *Track and Field*

Always have a goal. Whether short term or long, it will keep you motivated and focused on accomplishing that goal. – *Volleyball/ Softball*

If possible, get a roommate who doesn't have money problems, who is clean (or messy) like you, and don't put the bills in just one person's name. – *Baseball*

Have enough respect for the game and your team to always do and be your best. Abusing drugs and alcohol, not eating properly or getting enough sleep disrespects the sport, and your teammates/ coaching staff. – *Field Hockey*

Make friends with all sorts of different people. – *Soccer*

See the big picture and pay attention to little details along the way. Never lose sight of the mission. – *Volleyball/Basketball/Soccer*

Tell your loved ones how you feel about them because you never know what is going to happen to them. – *Diving*

I never realized how being the leader of my team motivated ME to work harder. I tried to make my team better by pushing them and setting high standards, but never knew that having them to push made me so much better too. Always trying to set the example, actually made it easier for me to succeed because working hard was expected. - *Volleyball*

Obstacles overcome and how we did it

Acute homesickness, for lack of a better phrase. I've always been surrounded by family and good friends and beginning my new life in college far away from my home and the security of family and friends was very difficult. It took two years for me to feel comfortable, secure and confident "being alone". I made it through with the support of administrators and my coaches. - *Softball*

Learned how to properly manage and budget my money. Sounds simple, but keeping my checkbook balanced and debit card purchases down was very difficult. Realize that the money on your (credit/debit) card is real money! – *Cross Country/Track and Field*

Overcame the "fear" to lead a group. This can be done by support and practice. – *Basketball*

There weren't many positive role models for me where I grew up so I listened to my parents and chose what information to listen to from others. – *Track and Field/Cross Country*

Being in a new place. Having a team is like a family away from home. It helps to develop relationships like this. – *Soccer*

At first I hated that my team watched me so closely, but now I know that I represent more than just myself. – *Swimming*

Roommate problems – I was more open to change and more open with how I felt. – *Track and Field/Cross Country*

Just struggling with having a hectic schedule, not getting enough sleep, being way too stressed because of an overload of events, activities and organizations I was involved in. I was trying to do too much which was affecting my health, well-being and my sport. I decided to schedule less in a day and not to overflow my plate every day. – *Volleyball*

Taking care of your body is something that is not too difficult but it does take planning and attention. So take the time to figure out when you're going to eat, when you're going to sleep and when you're going to study and then stick with it. – *Diving*

The slow process of separating my ideas from my parents. – *Basketball*

Managing sleep, eating, training… I had to get a planner and make sure I got everything done. – *Volleyball*

Scholarship checks don't go very far. I went from being very irresponsible with money to being able to balance my budget fairly well by keeping in mind that the last 2 weeks of each month are equally important as the first 2 and I need to be able to eat all month long! I stopped eating out so much and stopped buying things that weren't all that important. – *Football*

Peer pressure – you must have confidence in yourself and be independent. – *Soccer*

My issues with food. After I lost a lot of weight, I thought I would be happy inside, but I really wasn't. I wasted SO much time and energy, that could have been spent on other things, worrying about something that is so minor, really. It was a whirlwind of confusion and I felt VERY alone. Finally, I realized that my family and friends love me for who I am, not what I look like. - *Volleyball*

Minor obstacle with eating habits and teammates. We discussed their comments in a casual setting. – *Golf*

Gained way too much weight due to eating as a result of stress. I let God take control; became more disciplined in that respect. – *Volleyball*

I had to take make hard decisions, such as take care of my body, not party, and get sleep, because it will make my performance better. – *Basketball*

Adjusting to a new environment, peer pressure, and individuality. – *Soccer*

Confidence – my level was very low and my coach helped me to believe in my abilities. – *Equestrian*

Hazing – You don't have to participate to be part of the team. Make good choices. Don't do something that will affect how you represent the university or your team. – *Basketball*

Trying not to get sucked into the social scene. Surround yourself with people that have the same goals. – *Football*

Health problems and emotional stresses. I had a great family and friends to help. – *Volleyball*

Being 3,000 miles from home. I made great friends who took my mind off being homesick. – *Soccer*

My extreme shyness and fear of failure. I took risks and (decided) "don't worry be happy." – *Basketball*

I come from a town of about 420 people and moved to (college) where the campus is 23,500. It was a slight adjustment, but athletics helped. It helped because athletics in itself is much like a small community, everybody knows you and you know them. It is a great feeling. – *Volleyball/Basketball/Soccer*

Best thing I ever did for myself in this area

Got involved in the Student-Athlete Advisory Committee. SAAC completely changed my life in a number of ways. It opened the door for so many tremendous opportunities. It also gave me some outstanding experiences that enhanced my life and that can serve as a tangible benefit that looks great on a resume. - *Football*

I opened myself up to the members of my team. This allowed me to have some of the best experiences of my life. – *Tennis*

Coming to the conclusion that my past successes and previous operational methods would not suffice when future problems arose. - *Track and Field*

Not be shaken in pressure moments. – *Volleyball*

Focused more on school and athletics over the social scene of alcohol and going out until all hours. I learned that drinking was not helping my game. – *Basketball*

Met with a nutritionist on a regular basis. This got my health and my fitness organized and controllable. – *Soccer*

Worked very hard in the off season and ate right; as a result I returned to camp in the best shape I've ever been in. – *Football*

I was involved in many leadership groups, which opened the door for other opportunities. These are things I feel privileged to have been part of, mostly because of what they stand for. They embody the true college academic experience of gaining knowledge and wisdom. – *Golf*

Never gave up. Learned from each experience. – *Ice Hockey*

Worked on me first, and then I was able to help others. – *Basketball*

Used defeat as a learning tool, as well as a motivator. – *Track and Field*

Sought out personal mentors on campus, within athletics and in the community. – *Volleyball/Basketball/Soccer*

Practicing self-discipline in these areas saved me from problems. – *Track and Field*

Created a personal budget monthly. – *Volleyball*

Never succumbed to peer pressure. Stayed focused and kept my priorities in order. – *Soccer*

Found other new passions like volunteering and dancing, that proved to provide relaxation, and a break from studies. – *Golf*

Pushed through the challenging times where I just wanted to give up. – *Volleyball*

Made myself become a better communicator. I had to come out of my shell. I've gone from being a little shy freshman, who wouldn't even look her coach in the eye, to a take charge senior... – *Basketball*

Stood my ground on my old-fashioned choices; shows who your real friends are and what you believe to be important. – *Track and Field/Cross Country*

Be sure that I put something fun in when I had a lot of work to do, to break monotony and to keep stress down. – *Track and Field*

Throughout my college career, I have found that if I keep myself out of places I know I shouldn't be, then I can't get in trouble. – *Basketball*

My outlet was a Christian organization on campus, which filled the spiritual side of my life and gave me other social opportunities. – *Golf*

Developing a mature outlook as a freshman and remaining focused. – *Basketball*

I was involved in many different groups on campus – not just athletically or academically. – *Baseball*

Applied for the leadership program. – *Swimming*

Made lots of great friends, learned to study hard and managed my time. – *Soccer*

I wasn't too infatuated with the social events that accompany college life. I allowed myself to focus on my studies and my sport and realized that these things will always come first. – *Tennis*

I mentored a younger student-athlete to become the leader/ captain after I left. – *Basketball*

Our competitors have praised our team for having good sportsmanship. Since we treat each other with respect at practice, it carries over to our attitude during races. – *Crew*

Assessment

WHERE ARE YOU?
WHERE DO YOU WANT TO GO?
HOW WILL YOU GET THERE?

1. Identify your goals in personal development (short term/long term).

   a. Health and Wellness
   b. Leadership and Character
   c. Essential Life Skills

2. Are you truly committed to achieving these goals?

3. Are your daily activities congruent with your goals and values?

4. What skill set is necessary for success in personal development and which can you improve/develop?

   a. Health and Wellness
   b. Leadership and Character
   c. Essential Life Skills

5. Identify the changes, challenges and choices you have had to make in this area.

   a. Health and Wellness
   b. Leadership and Character
   c. Essential Life Skills

6. What are your assumptions in personal development? Are they accurate? What is something you were sure of in personal development that you aren't sure of anymore?

   a. Health and Wellness
   b. Leadership and Character
   c. Essential Life Skills

7. Identify opportunities and resources (on campus and in the athletics department) in this area?

   a. Health and Wellness
   b. Leadership and Character
   c. Essential Life Skills

8. What are things you can/can't control in this area?

   a. Health and Wellness
   b. Leadership and Character
   c. Essential Life Skills

9. Who is your circle of influence and support system?

10. How are you contributing to or taking away from your personal development accomplishments?

11. When are communication skills important in personal development and how would you rate yourself?

12. With which quotes could you relate to the most and why?

13. How many activities or groups are you involved in outside of your team?

14. Do you actively seek friends outside of athletics?

15. Do you feel well-versed in personal development issues listed in the different sections? On which topics would you like more information?

16. Consider who you are – who you really are at your core. Do you have the courage to be that person at all times and in all circumstances? When might you be tested?

17. What 3-5 experiences or people have had the most impact on your life? How and why? To what extent has your involvement in sports made you the person you are today?

18. What preventative measures do you take to stay safe if you are out partying? (designated driver, alternating drinks, eating, etc.)

19. What role do you think the media (TV, movies, magazines etc.) plays in the following and how does it affect your perception/attitudes?

   a. Violence/Aggression
   b. Body image
   c. Sexual expression
   d. What it means to be a "man"

20. What would you consider to be your greatest character strength?

21. What are your unique talents?

22. How would a coach or teammate describe your attitude in general?

23. If you could be, do, or achieve anything before you graduate, what would those things be?

24. Billy Mills, 1964 gold medalist in the 10,000 and Native American, says the greatest challenge we face in a changing world is perceptions. Would you agree? How does that relate to your life experiences?

25. Do you understand credit card issues, interest rates, compounding interest and other basic financial management issues?

26. If you are in a relationship, how well do you REALLY know your partner and their past? How well do you know your own body?

27. Rate your time management skills. What is ONE thing you could do better in this area, starting today?

28. Check out the list of issues identified by student-athletes on pages 27-28. Which of these are a concern of yours?

29. Are you aware of sound nutritional habits? What issues are there for you in the dorms, on campus, on the road? (See the Gatorade website at www.gssiweb.com for some great sports nutrition information. Courtesy of Gatorade Sport Science Institute).

30. Are you an emotional eater? Drinker? Spender? What are your triggers? What are some things you could do to prevent a trigger from happening or to help next time it happens?

31. How does health relate to performance? Are you doing all you can to be at your best?

32. How well do you deal with stress in your life – emotionally, behaviorally or cognitively? Is anger an issue for you? Name 3 outlets you have.

33. Do you know where your counseling center is on campus? Freshman Year Center?

34. Do you know which over the counter supplements would make you test positive on a drug test? (Check with your trainer).

35. Are you getting enough sleep? How many hours a night is optimal for you?

36. Do you know hazing is illegal in some states? Does your team engage in anything that might be considered hazing?

37. Evaluate your written, verbal, and non-verbal communication skills. How could you improve them?

38. Have you had to deal with grief or loss in your life? What impact has that had on you?

39. Ethical standards and practices are major issues today. What ethical dilemmas have you faced and how did you deal with them?

40. Would you care if what you did last night were on the front page of the newspaper today?

41. The NCAA uses Koucez/Posner's Leadership model of:
    - Challenging the Process
    - Inspiring a Shared Vision
    - Encouraging the Heart
    - Enabling Others to Act
    - Modeling the Way

    Also, many schools use Covey's 7 *Habits of Highly Effective People:*
    - Habit 1 – Be Proactive
    - Habit 2 – Begin with the End in Mind
    - Habit 3 – Put First Things First
    - Habit 4 – Think Win-Win
    - Habit 5 – Seek First to Understand, Then to Be Understood
    - Habit 6 - Synergize
    - Habit 7 – Sharpen the Saw

Think about the leadership models just mentioned. What do you do on a daily basis in these areas? What are your contributions to your team? What are some leadership groups with which you might want to get involved within athletics or on campus? (See your CHAMPS coordinator to get more information and to do an assessment of your leadership skills.)

P-Factor Analysis

➢ **Personalization**

(Setting personal development goals and strategies to achieve them; determining priorities; taking initiative; building a personal development support system and positive circle of influence; daily choices; self-responsibility and discipline; courage in defining moments; communication skills; staying true to yourself. **Examples:** eating well; sleeping enough; representing your team and university well; budgeting your money; making healthy choices; seeking leadership opportunities; doing assessments to understand personal preferences, etc.)

- What can I start doing today in the personal development area? (Health and Wellness; Leadership and Character; Essential Life Skills).
- What can I stop doing?
- What can I continue doing?
- How would I rate myself on a scale of 1-10 in personal development personalization? _____
- Who can help me in this area?

➢ **Preparation**

(Developing a personal development skill set; preparation (based on priorities) for day-to-day tasks and over time; implementing strategies; time management; organization/planning; attention to detail; going above and beyond; quality training; gaining experience; developing capacity in physical, emotional, mental and spiritual components. **Examples:** attending workshops and seminars on various topics; planning out your day; being well-rounded; building solid character traits, etc.)

- What can I start doing today?
- What can I stop doing?
- What can I continue doing?

- How would I rate myself on a scale of 1-10 in personal development preparation? _____
- Who can help me in this area?

➤ **Process**

(Day-to-day actions and behaviors in relation to personal development goals and congruent with stated values and priorities; being fully engaged; staying focused on present task and relevant cues; practicing skills; looking at "how" you do what you do; consistency in the fundamental process. **Examples:** daily eating, sleeping, spending habits; daily manners and etiquette; daily communication; daily health and wellness choices, etc.)

- What can I start doing today?
- What can I stop doing?
- What can I continue doing?
- How would I rate myself on a scale of 1-10 in personal development process? _____
- Who can help me in this area?

➤ **Problem Solving**

(Analyzing root of problem; asking for help early if you need it; utilizing campus/ ICA resources, enlisting help of support system; examining/reassessing your strategies, approach and daily process; developing and identifying options (Plan B); seeking win-win solutions with respect, cooperation, communication, commitment. **Examples:** making an appointment to meet with someone in problem area; researching information on problem topics; talking it out; making positive choices in defining moments, etc.)

- What can I start doing today?
- What can I stop doing?
- What can I continue doing?
- How would I rate myself on a scale of 1-10 in personal development problem solving? _____
- Who can help me in this area?

➤ **Persistence**

(Staying committed and focused on goals; being determined; being resilient; working through difficult and challenging times. **Examples:** displaying patience and continuing to develop and work toward goals in target areas, etc.)

- What can I start doing today?
- What can I stop doing?
- What can I continue doing?
- How would I rate myself on a scale of 1-10 in personal development persistence? _____
- Who can help me in this area?

➢ **Perspective**

(Confirming/reassessing assumptions; seeing the big picture; being open to other points of view; looking at frame of reference and interpretation of events; learning from each experience; having a positive attitude. **Examples:** accepting/appreciating teammates/roommates/people that are different than you; learning from experiences, etc.)

- What can I start doing today?
- What can I stop doing?
- What can I continue doing?
- How would I rate myself on a scale of 1-10 in personal development perspective? _____
- Who can help me in this area?

➢ **Pause**

(Relaxation; reflection; appreciation. **Examples:** taking time to relax, regroup, distress; accepting who you (and others) are; anticipating how to handle different situations that may arise; reflecting on how significant people and events have shaped your life; discovering your passion and purpose, etc.)

- What can I start doing today?
- What can I stop doing?
- What can I continue doing?
- How would I rate myself on a scale of 1-10 in personal development pausing? _____
- Who can help me in this area?

OVERALL SCORE FOR PERSONAL DEVELOPMENT: _____

Make The Commitment To Personal Development!

Game Plan

Career Development

Explore your options

Start early! **Network!**

Find a mentor

Do your resume

Use the career center

Find your passion

Attend info sessions

Get internships

Career Development

Top pieces of advice:

1. Do internships.
2. Find your passion and pursue it.
3. Use the career center on campus.
4. Attend info sessions.
5. Network, network, network!
6. Do assessments to help determine what you might like to do.
7. Do your resume early in your career.
8. Join clubs and organizations in your field.
9. Do what YOU want, not what others want you to do.
10. Use the gen-ed classes to see what possibilities are out there. Research, explore your options!
11. Talk to professors/advisors for guidance.
12. Find a mentor in your field.
13. Develop a strong foundation for a resume (in terms of education, skills and experiences).

If we had it to do all over again we would have:

1. Done an internship or gotten involved in other things to put on my resume.
2. Started planning sooner in my career.
3. Been involved in leadership groups.
4. Been open to more ideas about what I could do.
5. Done my resume sooner.

6. Utilized the campus career center.

7. Networked more!

8. Researched majors/careers more before deciding.

General Thoughts

Network – find people that will help you. Keep talking to others and eventually down the chain, there will be someone who will change your life. – *Alpine Skiing*

Explore every opportunity that you encounter – you never know what might spark your interest. You never want to look back and wonder, "What If…" - *Diving*

The internship I did was a great opportunity. The experience helped me develop confidence in all areas - from sport, to academic, to community involvement. – *Soccer*

Try to take classes outside of your major. Just because you don't need it, doesn't mean it can't help you. Many of today's jobs are not restricted to just one field of study. You can benefit by having a background in other areas. It will make you more marketable. – *Volleyball/Softball*

Use athletics to propel you in the direction you want to go. Use the tools learned from being on a team and competing. They are very helpful in real life situations. – *Lacrosse*

You don't have to know what you're going to do with your life to be in college. Universities will help you solve that problem. – *Basketball*

Get internships early and often. – *Volleyball*

Be realistic. Understand that everyone is not capable of playing professionally and you should have other options. – *Track and Field*

Instead of looking at Gen-Ed's as requirements, think of them as possibilities to explore what you might want to do. - *Diving*

Research, research, research. Use your resources and start researching what you like and different areas. - *Track and Field*

Get to know professors, administrators, coaches, etc., that can inform you and help you become knowledgeable about different fields. – *Volleyball*

Social skills become as important as scholastic skills. – *Track and Field*

Take classes in a manageable timetable for you. You can have extra time for education. Get the most out of everything you do. – *Soccer*

Find events or functions that deal with your field. – *Track and Field*

Spend a lot of time formulating a resume. – *Swimming*

Become well-rounded so you can pursue whatever career you wish (more options). – *Basketball*

You always think you can put things off and take care of it later. You think freshman year doesn't matter or you don't need to worry about career stuff til you're a senior. WRONG. Your freshman year grades count as much as any other, and with no experience it's much harder to get a job. – *Tennis*

Your work environment is identical to a team concept. – *Ice Hockey*

What you get your degree in may not be exactly what your first or second job is in. No job is beneath you. – *Diving*

Don't procrastinate on career searching and networking. If you do, someone else will hook up with your link and you will miss out. - *Volleyball*

Think ahead – the future is now. – *Softball*

Go to career/major fairs at your school to learn about different opportunities. – *Tennis*

Create experiences. Find hands-on experiences to help you grow. – *Volleyball*

Career choices are not set. If it's not something you like, get out. Courage is from change, not from sticking with something you despise. – *Track and Field/Cross Country*

You have it MADE when you're in college and on scholarship. They pay for EVERYTHING. Then you go out in the real world and it's like, YOU have to pay for it. Enjoy it while you can but be ready! – *Volleyball*

It's important that you seek out information on how to do a resume and how to interview well. Others are doing it and you can fall behind, without even knowing it. - *Track and Field*

If you're clueless, seek out people to talk to about everything you might be interested in. – *Volleyball*

Try to get an internship over a summer related to your field, to get your foot in the door. – *Tennis*

Don't wait until the month before you graduate to look for jobs and to network – do it as early as possible to give you more options. It's easy to forget about the real world while you are in school but it is out there and you need to be ready and prepared when it hits. – *Volleyball*

Build your resume with everything – jobs, community service, and volunteer work opportunities. – *Diving*

Try new things – maybe you're missing out on your true passion in life. – *Volleyball*

Your personality is, in part, molded through your every day experiences. Who you want to be and become changes relative to your personality. Allow for change and accept the person you are. Don't let your career define your personality; let your personality define your career. - *Swimming*

It's not only what you know, it's who you know. – *Soccer*

Network, network, network! People that you meet can help take you in a whole different direction and help you find your passion. – *Volleyball*

I told one employer I had over a 3.0. He told me they only interviewed people with over a 3.0! My extracurricular activities got me the job. – *Gymnastics*

If you don't know what you're interested in, find some different sorts of experiences/internships that can help you decide what you want to do. Many people waste their time pursuing a degree for an area that they completely dislike once they try it. – *Track and Field*

Be nice to geeks – chances are you'll be working for one someday! – *Soccer*

Use your career services center by the time the end of your junior year comes around. – *Volleyball*

Internships are a must. You may not learn anything or it may not be something you are interested in but when you apply for a job, and the employer sees "internship" on your resume, your resume immediately lights up and gets put in the "review/call for interview/job offer" pile. – *Volleyball/Softball*

Have an idea of what you want to do, but don't base your life around it. Have a back up plan. The consequences of not reaching a goal that you put everything into could be painful. - *Swimming*

Do not underestimate what it means to be a collegiate athlete and the transferable skills you have. – *Diving*

Find ways to participate in activities that will enhance your marketability in the workplace after graduation. – *Football*

Actively take an interest in your career development early in your college career, seek internships and service learning opportunities. – *Volleyball/Basketball/Soccer*

Don't limit yourself – participate in a wide variety of activities so that you can find your niche. – *Football*

Don't worry about what you are going to do after school too much. Try to do things during school that will help you be able to do WHATEVER is it you decide to do. – *Diving*

Obstacles overcome and how we did it

I started to get caught up in what others were doing that I wasn't in a major that I was actually happy in. I just had to refocus and remember my personal goals. – *Field Hockey*

I still don't know what my major is, so I am actively searching for ideas, opinions, and suggestions. – *Alpine Skiing*

People saying you can't...anyone can, and if you act, you will. – *Swimming*

Having a fear that I'm never going to find that one career which I love and am passionate about. I just need to be patient. – *Volleyball*

Choosing what I was truly interested in. I took a variety of different classes to see what appealed to me. I also talked to faculty about their areas of expertise to get more info. – *Field Hockey*

Finding interviews. To overcome this, I used our advisement center and the networking I had done throughout college. – *Track and Field*

Just realizing how important school is going to be in my career and working harder to get better grades. – *Football*

Realizing I was in the wrong major/on the wrong path. I had to admit my mistake, and get over the pride factor. – *Volleyball*

Hospitals don't hire people without experience. Medical schools don't accept students without hospital experience. I finally got a job through persistence, re-applying and a recommendation from a friend. – *Softball*

Surviving the stereotypes of being a black male in engineering. – *Track and Field*

Best thing I ever did for myself in this area

Developing a strong foundation in academics that gave me many different options when it was time to choose a career. – *Basketball*

Observed a class every day from 8:00am-3:00pm for two and a half weeks; learned essential lessons for becoming an effective teacher. – *Track and Field/Cross Country*

I took a lot of classes in what I thought I wanted to make my career in to make sure I liked it. – *Swimming*

I established new contacts in different areas every day. I searched for the elephants. – *Soccer*

I chose to use my 5th year (no athletics) to find out what I really wanted to do with my life. – *Basketball*

Kept my eyes open for alternative ideas, and kept an open mind about my interests. – *Lacrosse*

Experience a number of different jobs throughout my three summers, which is helping me determine my future plans. – *Track and Field*

I have built a foundation for a solid resume to help me when I get out of college. I have taken the risk of trying out many types of jobs and careers and have been involved in many career related activities and events. – *Volleyball*

Attending interview and resume writing seminars. – *Soccer*

Went to an advisor who told me so much information I didn't know. – *Track and Field*

Through hard work, and dedication, I received an offer for an internship this summer. It should provide me with a great opportunity to have my foot in the door with the industry. – *Swimming*

Got an internship in my area of concentration. Used my summer to go abroad and expand my education. – *Soccer*

Researched graduate programs and found the one I wanted. It gave me purpose and motivation with school, sports, and SAAC. – *Softball*

I wanted to have a feel for working in a Division 1 athletic department, so I drove 15 minutes down the road and ....walked right into the athletic office and asked to volunteer. I took the initiative to set up the internship for myself. This internship led to my being accepted for my Master's in sport management and allowed me to get a scholarship from the NCAA. - *Track and Field/Cross Country*

(Job) shadowed someone in the area I am interested in. – *Basketball*

Joined an organization in my field. – *Football*

Talked with my parents, coach, and academic advisors about what I want to do and how I go about doing it. – *Tennis*

Joined a related organization to my major which provided me a base of students I can talk to about schoolwork and form study groups with. – *Golf*

Went through the internship interview process and received a job offer in addition to an internship offer. - *Soccer*

I did my senior project on shadowing a surgeon resident. From this project I have learned so much about my field. – *Basketball*

Found an expert advisor in my field of interest who could matter-of-factly lay down the facts about the different professions in the medical field. Find someone who is willing to honestly discuss what a career is all about. – *Track and Field*

Worked in an area that will help me with my future career and allowed me to make sure my chosen field was what I imagined it to be. – *Softball*

Networked all over Africa, Europe and North America. – *Basketball*

Took on a major that I've always wanted to – regardless of how challenging it was. – *Tennis*

I could have worked at a clinic with my old high school trainer. It would have been a piece of cake – the interview would have been laid back, and relaxed and I would have felt more at ease. I did not take this option because I wanted to experience the stress of an interview, feel the pressure to perform and break into something totally new for once. I learned so much about myself and my abilities by just throwing myself to the wolves. I also got a bigger sense of accomplishment from doing it this way. Sometimes you need to be blinded in order to see more. - *Volleyball*

Joined clubs and organizations that deal with my career choice or help me increase skills that will prepare me for that career. – *Ice Hockey/Tennis*

Learned the importance of making plans and setting goals. – *Hockey*

Tried to be the speaker for groups at all times to get practice. – *Track and Field*

I did an assessment that gave me lots of ideas based on my interests and abilities. I still don't know exactly what I want to do but at least I have SOME direction! – *Gymnastics*

To find a career that I love and to pursue it with everything I have inside. As soon as I identified a possible path for my future, I began to prepare myself for success along this path. - *Football*

I had a paid internship during the summer of my freshman year. At first the work seemed boring and uninteresting. I didn't want to return the following summer. But I decided to go back and I worked at the company for the remaining summers of my college career. This past summer I was involved in doing exciting projects for the client and interacting with fellow employees on the same level. I realized that I had grown so much during the past summers and now I am looking at full time positions with the company. It really pays off to start getting experience early. If it doesn't help you decide what you want to do, it can help you decide what you aren't interesting in doing. - *Crew*

Assessment

WHERE ARE YOU?
WHERE DO YOU WANT TO GO?
HOW WILL YOU GET THERE?

1. Identify your goals in career development (short term/long term).

2. Are you truly committed to achieving these goals?

3. Are your daily activities congruent with your goals and values?

4. What skill set is necessary for success in career development and which can you improve/develop?

5. Identify the changes, challenges and choices you have had to face in this area.

6. What are your assumptions in career development? Are they accurate? What is something you were sure of in career development that you aren't sure of anymore?

7. Identify opportunities and resources (on campus and in the athletics department) in this area?

8. What are things you can/can't control in this area?

9. Who is your circle of influence and support system?

10. How are you contributing to or taking away from your career development accomplishments?

11. When are communication skills important in career development and how would you rate yourself?

12. With which quotes could you relate to the most and why?

13. Have you done any assessments in the areas of career interests, abilities and values and/or personality? (Strong Interest Inventory, Discover or SIGI, Self-Directed Search, Myers-Briggs Type Inventory? (Ask your life skills coordinator how you can sign up.) Based on your profile, these can help you consider what you may want to do in a career.

14. Do you want more information on particular career fields? (See the Bureau of Labor Statistics website at www.bls.gov/oco for great information about careers. Also, see www.jobhuntersbible.com for lots of helpful career links.)

15. One model lists the following 6 steps to career planning: Explore Yourself; Explore the World of Work; Make decisions and set goals; Plan your education; Obtain experience; Plan job search or grad school. Where are you in the process?

16. Do you have a year-by-year game plan for career development?

17. Does your school offer career fairs? Major fairs?

18. NACE (National Association of Colleges and Employers) has identified the following as the top qualities and skills employers look for in a candidate: Communication skills; Honesty/Integrity; Teamwork skills; Interpersonal skills; Motivation/Initiative; Strong work ethic; Analytical skills; Flexibility/Adaptability; Computer skills; Organizational skills; Detail oriented; Leadership skills; Self confidence. Identify your 3-5 best transferable skills?

19. Have you ever done a resume? What would/could you put on it?

20. Would you be comfortable in a job interview?

21. Why should you consider a summer internship?

22. With whom could you do an informational interview? Job Shadow? Why are these important?

23. Have you identified your work related values?

24. Are your familiar with your University's Career Center? What services do they provide that could benefit you?

25. Identify professional or campus organizations you could join in your field. (It's a great way to learn about or stay current with what's happening).

P-Factor Analysis

➤ **Personalization**

(Setting career development goals and strategies to achieve them; determining priorities; taking initiative; building a career development support system and positive circle of influence; daily choices; self-responsibility and discipline; courage in defining moments; communication skills. **Examples:** exploring your interests, values and abilities; learning about occupations and majors; talking to major/college advisors; developing relationships with faculty, advisors, counselors; starting career development early; getting involved in co-curricular activities, etc.)

- What can I start doing today?
- What can I stop doing?
- What can I continue doing?
- How would I rate myself on a scale of 1-10 in career development personalization? _____
- Who can help me in this area?

➤ **Preparation**

(Developing a career development/transferable skill set; preparation (based on priorities) for day-to-day tasks and over time; implementing strategies; time management; organization/ planning; attention to detail; going above and beyond; quality training; gaining experience; developing capacity in physical, emotional, mental and spiritual components. **Examples:** attending workshops, seminars, and career or major fairs; doing internships, job shadowing, summer jobs; getting good grades; developing contacts; using the career center; doing mock interviews; researching what is required in certain fields, having a 4 (or 5) year plan; joining organizations; reading journals in your field, etc.)

- What can I start doing today?
- What can I stop doing?
- What can I continue doing?
- How would I rate myself on a scale of 1-10 in career development preparation? _____
- Who can help me in this area?

➢ **Process**

(Daily or weekly actions and behaviors, and over time, in relation to career development goals and congruent with stated values and priorities; being fully engaged; staying focused on present task and relevant cues; practicing skills; looking at "how" you do what you do; consistency in the fundamental process. **Examples:** career development habits like checking job openings; continuing to network; updating your resume; staying up to date about your field; videotaping a mock interview, etc.)

- What can I start doing today?
- What can I stop doing?
- What can I continue doing?
- How would I rate myself on a scale of 1-10 in career development process? _____
- Who can help me in this area?

➢ **Problem Solving**

(Analyzing root of problem; asking for help early if you need it; utilizing campus/ ICA resources, enlisting help of support system; examining/reassessing your strategies, approach and daily process; developing and identifying options (Plan B); seeking win-win solutions with respect, cooperation, communication, commitment; **Examples:** making sure your qualifications meet job/internship description; evaluating resume, interviewing skills, job search strategies, etc.)

- What can I start doing today?
- What can I stop doing?
- What can I continue doing?
- How would I rate myself on a scale of 1-10 in career development problem solving? _____
- Who can help me in this area?

➢ **Persistence**

(Staying committed and focused on goals; being determined; being resilient; working through difficult and challenging times. **Examples:** keep trying if you don't get something the first time; let people know you are interested in a field/career/job; follow up; be enthusiastic; use contacts, etc.)

- What can I start doing today?
- What can I stop doing?
- What can I continue doing?
- How would I rate myself on a scale of 1-10 in career development persistence? _____
- Who can help me in this area?

➢ **Perspective**

(Confirming/reassessing assumptions; seeing the big picture; being open to other points of view; looking at frame of reference and interpretation of events; learning from each experience; having a positive attitude. **Examples:** understand job market and how/where you fit in; considering what jobs offer in terms of salary, work environments/demands, chance for advancement, and how that relates to your work values, etc.)

- What can I start doing today?
- What can I stop doing?
- What can I continue doing?
- How would I rate myself on a scale of 1-10 in career development perspective? _____
- Who can help me in this area?

➢ **Pause**

(Relaxation; reflection; appreciation. **Examples:** thinking about your passions – are you pursuing those things in a career, are you doing what YOU want, what do you want from a job, etc.)

- What can I start doing today?
- What can I stop doing?
- What can I continue doing?
- How would I rate myself on a scale of 1-10 in career development pausing? _____
- Who can help me in this area?

OVERALL SCORE FOR CAREER DEVELOPMENT: _____

Make The Commitment To Career Development!

Game Plan

Community Service

Get involved!

Change a life

Do stuff with your team

Get out of your comfort zone

Improve your speaking skills

Make a difference

Community Service

Top pieces of advice

1. Get involved!

2. Do stuff with your team.

3. Do things that are interesting to you.

4. Take time to realize what a difference you can make.

5. Find out about different opportunities and organizations with which you could get involved.

6. Get out of your comfort zone!

7. Keep a calendar of events so they don't pass you by.

8. Do different kinds of community service.

If we had it to do all over again we would have:

1. Done more.

2. Done it earlier.

3. Come up with new and fun activities to make the community know that we're there.

4. Get involved with an organization and make a commitment for a period of time. (To really make a difference in a child's life).

5. Tried harder to get my team involved.

6. Organized my schedule so I could do more.

General Thoughts

My community service has helped me tons, due to getting out there and speaking up. Those experiences helped me all the way down to just introducing myself, how I carried myself, and when it came down to talking with my boss, or presenting ideas, I was more comfortable within the atmosphere of having people in front of me, waiting to hear what I had to say. Overall, the experience of going out of my comfort zone, challenged me to step up, and follow through. It helped me on the field, in the classroom, and overall gave me an experience that was worth being uncomfortable at first, and working my way through it. - *Soccer*

Small gestures can go a long way. – *Softball*

Groups of friends will always be interested in activities where they can spend time together. – *Soccer*

Seek for those who need help. Needy people are not always obvious. – *Track and Field*

These are the things people will remember you for, more so than athletics, I believe. Go out into the community and let people see you as a person. It's good for them to see you out of your uniform, in day-to-day life. - *Basketball*

Community service allows you to become more well-rounded. – *Swimming*

I love participating in community service and I hope to make it a large part of my professional life as well. - *Football*

Get your feet wet and you're in (the first time is the key!) – *Baseball*

You may think you don't have time, but you just have to be creative. – *Field Hockey*

Speaking in public always kind of scared me. I found out that the best audience is elementary school children. You can talk to them about anything and they will be happy just to have you in the same room. They will tell you stories and ask questions. They don't judge you. They smile. They are the perfect audience. - *Diving*

You need to remember that it is the little things that matter. Even one smile can greatly change a child's life. – *Soccer*

Someone once gave to you, so you should continue the process. – *Track and Field*

Do charity work or community service. You feel a lot better about yourself and it really does carry over to your performance in the classroom and on the playing field. – *Baseball*

Don't be too cool for community service. – *Football*

You are the role model – remember when you were little what you felt like when you saw your role models? – *Volleyball*

Think outside your school bubble. – *Softball*

Community service brings you together as athletic teams – it provides unity, and a sense of team pride. – *Track and Field/Cross Country*

In an internship I did, I had to speak in front of 250 adults (without warning!) about a project we were working on. First of all, I didn't have time to get nervous, but also, because of all my community service speaking, I felt pretty comfortable. It probably would have been WAY worse if I hadn't had those experiences! – *Track and Field*

Don't think something doesn't matter. – *Soccer*

Don't be self centered and only concerned with your future. You probably didn't obtain your success alone; help others to make the journey also. If no one else wants to give, do it by yourself – it only takes one. - *Track and Field*

Community service teaches you about things outside your comfort zone. – *Tennis*

Helping others is the best dose of humility. – *Basketball*

There is nothing like the feeling of doing community service. – *Wrestling*

Make it a point to help others just by being nice – kids will look up to you and adults will respect you. – *Basketball*

...the little kids especially look up to athletes. Kids have some of the greatest questions and sometimes they really make you stop and think about what it is that you are doing. - *Track and Field*

I loved every single minute of it. It is something different to do and you learn so much from the community. – *Volleyball*

He who gives selflessly will receive so much more than he expected in return. – *Track and Field*

Do you know what it feels like to be out somewhere in a store or restaurant and to have a bunch of little kids come up to you and ask for your autograph? – *Volleyball*

Community service does not have to be a full time commitment. There are all sorts of small, isolated events that are fulfilling. Saying you don't have enough time for it is NOT a valid excuse. – *Track and Field*

Helping others often has a more profound effect on you than on those you help. – *Softball*

This can be one of the best things to do to get your mind off of school, off of work, off of your sport, and even off of YOURSELF. You are doing something for someone else, and it will be so rewarding for you and them – even if you don't know it. - *Diving*

Start public speaking as early as possible. – *Soccer/Softball*

Do something you never thought you'd be able to do and surprise yourself when you succeed. – *Field Hockey*

I never regret prioritizing helping others over my own personal time. – *Volleyball*

Children are the key to our future. – *Basketball*

Don't do community service just because it looks good or because someone else wants you to be there. When you are doing it, know that it can be an incredible experience if you really let it be. – *Track and Field*

You live once – make a difference. – *Softball*

Do what you can – many applications ask for experiences. – *Golf*

Employers look for community service. – *Volleyball*

Be outgoing and friendly. A lot of times people (especially children) are intimidated by athletes. Go up to them and start a conversation. It will make the whole process easier. – *Baseball*

Have fun when you do it and others will follow. – *Basketball*

Obstacles overcome and how we did it

Finding time to get involved – I wrote out a schedule and put community service on paper and in my schedule. – *Track and Field*

Time – but you just need to make the time. You'll never find it, you just have to make it. – *Tennis*

We have a hard time getting a diverse group to volunteer. It's often the same group over and over. However, we'll overcome that by sharing how good our experiences were. *Track and Field/Cross Country*

Pubic speaking – being shy. How I got over it is practice. One thing I do is look past the crowd – behind them. This way it looks like you are looking at the whole group, but really you are looking at the wall behind them. After awhile you start looking at the people and it doesn't bother you as much. *– Soccer/Volleyball*

Getting people to actually get together and do it – but after one time, everybody will be eager to do it again. *– Basketball*

I didn't volunteer as much as I should have. I had more time than I thought. I put a lot of unnecessary pressure on myself. I am a stress – ball! *– Volleyball*

I got too nervous when I talked. Now I just don't care anymore because others feel the same way. *– Track and Field*

Best thing I ever did for myself in this area

Talk to younger students about athletics or help older people in nursing homes because it's a completely different high than winning a game or race. Knowing you helped make a difference in someone's life is an incredible feeling. *– Track and Field*

Team organized programs are so rewarding and so much fun. My team lead a program called "Character Coaching" where we visited an elementary class weekly and talked about the six pillars of good character. *– Soccer*

Going and seeing kids being influenced by athletes and getting them to dream higher and be active was great. *– Swimming*

Got very involved in dance lessons and volunteering at a local daycare. It was a great break from school and golf. I met new friends and had new experiences. *– Golf*

I volunteer at a home for children and I know that for that hour, each week these kids were happy. *– Soccer*

I have learned to voice my opinion, and communicate effectively amongst people I never knew. *- Tennis*

Maintained a constant relationship with the members of whatever community I am surrounded by because I understand the privileged position that I am in. – *Track and Field*

Asked how I can get involved. – *Soccer*

I took the time to understand that community service is an integral part of being an athlete – (or someone well known in the community.) – *Basketball*

The feeling of building a house is priceless. – *Track and Field/Cross Country*

I was able to volunteer and experience what I take for granted. – *Tennis*

I took an active role in the planning and implementation of several community service projects. - *Football*

Special Olympic athletes have truly been an inspiration to me. They make me work hard. – *Track and Field/Cross Country*

Joined a sorority that does lots of work for breast cancer awareness. – *Soccer*

Got involved in activities that are both leadership and community service. Doing something for somebody else that is in need is the absolute BEST thing you could do with your time. You will meet great people and do life-changing activities. – *Track and Field*

Assessment

WHERE ARE YOU?
WHERE DO YOU WANT TO GO?
HOW WILL YOU GET THERE?

1. Identify your goals in community service (short term/long term).

2. Are you truly committed to achieving these goals?

3. Are your daily activities congruent with your goals and values?

4. What skill set is necessary for success in community service and which can you improve/develop?

5. Identify the changes, challenges and choices you have had to face in this area.

6. What are your assumptions for community service? Are they accurate? What is something you were sure of in community service that you aren't sure of anymore?

7. Identify opportunities and resources (on campus and in the athletics department) in this area?

8. What are things you can/can't control in this area?

9. Who is your circle of influence and support system?

10. How are you contributing to or taking away from your community service accomplishments?

11. When are communication skills important in community service and how would you rate yourself?

12. With which quotes could you relate to the most and why?

13. Are you comfortable doing public speaking?

14. Name three benefits to doing community service?

15. Are you willing to go out of your comfort zone?

16. Who were/are your role models and why?

17. How does being involved in community service activities change your perspective or affect other areas of your life?

18. For which cause or charitable organization do you have an interest? How can you contribute?

P-Factor Analysis

➤ **Personalization**

(Setting community service goals and strategies to achieve them; determining priorities; taking initiative; building a community service support system and positive circle of influence; daily choices; self-responsibility and discipline; courage in defining moments; communication skills. **Examples:** get involved; ask about different opportunities/activities with different organizations; get your team involved, etc.)

- What can I start doing today in the community service area?
- What can I stop doing?
- What can I continue doing?
- How would I rate myself on a scale of 1-10 in community service personalization? _____
- Who can help me in this area?

➤ **Preparation**

(Developing a community service (including public speaking) skill set; preparation (based on priorities) for day-to-day tasks and over time; implementing strategies; time management; organization/ planning; attention to detail; going above and beyond; quality training; gaining experience; developing capacity in physical, emotional, mental and spiritual components. **Examples:** know the group to which you will be speaking; what your topic will be; develop a talk track you want to follow, etc.)

- What can I start doing today?
- What can I stop doing?
- What can I continue doing?
- How would I rate myself on a scale of 1-10 in community service preparation? _____
- Who can help me in this area?

CHAPTER 9 **Community Service** 131

➢ **Process**

(Day-to-day actions and behaviors, and over time, in relation to community service goals and congruent with stated values and priorities; being fully engaged; staying focused on present task and relevant cues; practicing skills; looking at "how" you do what you do; consistency in the fundamental process. **Examples:** analyzing speaking habits (grammar, fillers, etc.), doing community service appearances; practicing speaking skills whenever you can (class, groups); videotaping a speaking appearance, etc.)

- What can I start doing today?
- What can I stop doing?
- What can I continue doing?
- How would I rate myself on a scale of 1-10 in community service process? _____
- Who can help me in this area?

➢ **Problem Solving**

(Analyzing root of problem; asking for help early if you need it; utilizing campus/ ICA resources, enlisting help of support system; examining/reassessing your strategies, approach and daily process; developing and identifying options (Plan B); seeking win-win solutions with respect, cooperation, communication, commitment. **Examples:** practice, practice, practice; analyzing videotape or recording; having relevant topic and speaking to level of audience, etc.)

- What can I start doing today?
- What can I stop doing?
- What can I continue doing?
- How would I rate myself on a scale of 1-10 in community service problem solving? _____
- Who can help me in this area?

➢ **Persistence**

(Staying committed and focused on goals; being determined; being resilient; working through difficult or challenging times. **Examples:** keep doing it – you will become better, more comfortable over time; practice with different sized groups, etc.)

- What can I start doing today?

- What can I stop doing?
- What can I continue doing?
- How would I rate myself on a scale of 1-10 in community service persistence? _____
- Who can help me in this area?

➤ **Perspective**

(Confirming/reassessing assumptions; seeing the big picture; being open to other points of view; looking at frame of reference and interpretation of events; learning from each experience; having a positive attitude. **Examples:** understand how speaking skills impact other areas of your life; compassion for those less fortunate; experience different kinds of community service, etc.)

- What can I start doing today?
- What can I stop doing?
- What can I continue doing?
- How would I rate myself on a scale of 1-10 in community service perspective? _____
- Who can help me in this area?

➤ **Pause**

(Relaxation; reflection; appreciation. **Examples:** consider the impact you could make in someone's life; think of the message you are sending - what that means to you, and how that plays out in your own life; considering how fortunate you are; appreciating what you have, etc.)

- What can I start doing today?
- What can I stop doing?
- What can I continue doing?
- How would I rate myself on a scale of 1-10 in community service pausing? _____
- Who can help me in this area?

OVERALL SCORE FOR COMMUNITY SERVICE: _____

Make The Commitment To Community Service!

Game Plan

Reasons For Our Success

Hard work

Time management

Discipline

Persistence

Focus

setting goals

Positive attitude

Reasons for our success

1. Hard work/Preparation

2. Setting goals

3. Determination

4. Discipline

5. Support System

6. Persistence

7. Time management

8. Communication

9. Being true to ourselves and our values

10. Commitment/Dedication

11. Focus

12. Positive attitude

13. God/Faith

14. Having fun/enjoying what we do

15. Effort – giving 100%

16. Passion

17. Respect – for ourselves and others

A Final Thought

As we can see from what the student-athletes have told us, success revolves around many things. Let me pick one more, courage, to embrace the ideals of the others, in this wish for you.

I wish for you the:

Courage to do what's right and the
Courage to change what's wrong

Courage to keep going and the
Courage to change directions

Courage to take action and the
Courage to do nothing

Courage to ask for what you need and the
Courage to give as much as you can

Courage to admit a mistake and the
Courage to accept an apology

Courage to take risks and the
Courage to understand the odds

Courage to leave your comfort zone and the
Courage to stay true to yourself

THE COURAGE TO COMMIT TO YOURSELF

Good luck to you in all that you do.

Berly Bell

CHAMPS
Programs of Excellence
Awarded by the Division 1A
Athletics Directors Association

In 1997, the Division 1A Athletics Directors Association began
recognizing universities that showed proven excellence in all five
areas of CHAMPS. Here is a list of the recipients to date.

1997-1998

North Carolina State University
The Ohio State University
University of Arizona – www.u.arizona.edu/~cats
University of Texas - Austin

1998-1999

Florida State University
Penn State University
Syracuse University
University of Florida
University of Nebraska
University of Oklahoma
University of Washington

1999-2000

University of Alabama
Clemson University
University of Georgia
Georgia Technical Institute
University of Kentucky
University of Tennessee

2000-2001

Arizona State University
University of Iowa
Michigan State University
University of Notre Dame

2001-2002

Ball State University
Central Michigan University
Louisiana State University

2002-2003

Brigham Young University
University of Missouri
University of Oregon

For more specific information on these, or other programs, you can access their websites using a search engine like Yahoo.

List Of
Participating Schools

Thank you to the student-athletes from the following schools who contributed quotes for this book:

Albion College

Appalachian State University

Arizona State University

Augsburg College

Belmont University

Boston University

Bridgewater State College

Brigham Young University

Cabrini College

California State University, Fresno

California University of Pennsylvania

Canisius College

Carthage College

Castleton State College

Central Missouri State University

Cleveland State University

Colgate University

College of St. Benedict/St.John's University

Columbia University

Duquesne University

Eastern Illinois University

Eastern Michigan University

Eastern College

Eastern Washington University

Elizabeth City State University

Fitchburg State College

Florida State University

Illinois Wesleyan University

Indiana State University

Indiana University of Pennsylvania

Iona College

Kent State University

LaSalle University

Long Island University -Brooklyn Campus

Louisiana Tech University

Loyola Marymount University

Manhattanville College

Mansfield University of Pennsylvania

Michigan State University

Missouri Southern State College

Monmouth University

Morgan State University

Mount Holyoke College

Mt. Saint Mary's College

North Carolina A&T State University

North Carolina State University

North Dakota State University

Northern Arizona University

Northern Illinois University

Northwood University

Oklahoma State University

Old Dominion University

Pennsylvania State University

Portland State University

Providence College

Purdue University

Regis University

Salisbury University

Samford University

Santa Clara University

Seton Hall University

Southeastern Louisiana University

Southern Illinois University, Edwardsville

Springfield College

St. Cloud State University

St. Francis University (Pennsylvania)

St. Peter's College

State University College at Cortland

State University College at New Paltz

State University of New York Institute of Technology at Utica/Rome

State University College at Oswego

Stephen F. Austin State University

Stevens Institute of Technology

Syracuse University

Temple University

Texas A&M University Kingsville

Truman State University

Tulane University

United States Air Force Academy

University of Akron

University of Alabama at Birmingham

University of Alabama - Tuscaloosa

University of Arizona

University of Arkansas, Fayetteville

University of California Riverside

University of Cincinnati

University of Colorado, Boulder

University of Dayton

University of Denver

University of Evansville
University of Georgia
University of Hawaii
University of Idaho
University of Illinois - Urbana Champaign
University of Kentucky
University of Louisville
University of Maryland, Eastern Shore
University of Miami (Florida)
University of Missouri
University of Nebraska Omaha
University of New Hampshire
University of New Orleans
University of North Carolina Charlotte
University of North Carolina Greensboro
University of Oklahoma
University of Oregon
University of Rhode Island
University of San Diego
University of South Carolina, Columbia
University of South Carolina, Spartanburg
University of Southern Maine
University of Texas - Austin
University of Utah
University of Virginia
University of Washington
University of Wyoming
University of Delaware
Valparaiso University
Virginia Polytechnic Institute and State University
Wake Forest University
Washington College (Maryland)

Weber State University
West Texas A&M University
Western Carolina University
Wichita State University
Wilimington College (Ohio)
Wittenberg University

Recommended Reading

Mitch Albom, *Tuesday's With Morrie* (New York: Doubleday, 1997).

Lance Armstrong with Sally Jenkins, *It's Not About the Bike – My Journey Back to Life* (New York: Berkley Publishing Group, 2000).

Warren Bennis and Burt Namus, *Leaders* (New York: Harper and Row, 1985).

Richard N. Bolles, *What Color is Your Parachute?* (Berkeley: Ten Speed Press, 2000).

Nathaniel Branden, *The Six Pillars Of Self Esteem* (New York: Bantam Books, 1994).

Stephen R. Covey, *The Seven Habits of Highly Effective People* (New York: Simon & Schuster, 1989).

Stephen R. Covey, *Principled Centered Leadership* (New York: Simon & Schuster, 1990).

Michael J. Gelb, *How To Think Like Leonardo DaVinci* (New York: Dell Publishing, 1998).

Daniel Goleman, *Emotional Intelligence* (New York: Bantam Books, 1995).

Spencer Johnson, *Who Moved My Cheese?* (G.P. Putnam's Son's, 1998).

James M. Kouzes, and Barry A. Posner, *The Leadership Challenge* (San Francisco: Jossey-Bass Publishers, 1995).

Dr. James Loehr, *Stress for Success* (Times Books, 1998).

Dr. James Loehr, *The Power of Full Engagement* (Due 2003).

John C. Maxwell, *Your Road Map for Success* (Nashville: Thomas Nelson Publishers, 2002).

John C. Maxwell, *The 21 Irrefutable Laws of Leadership* (Nashville: Thomas Nelson Publishers, 1998).

Dr. Phillip McGraw, *Self Matters* (New York: Simon & Schuster, 2001).

M. Scott Peck, *The Road Less Traveled* (New York: Simon & Schuster, 1978).

Martin Seligman, *Learned Optimism* (New York: Pocket Books, 1990).

Paul D. Tieger, and Barbara Baron Tieger, *Do What You Are* (Boston: Little, Brown and Company, 1992).

John Wooden and Jack Tobin, *They Call Me Coach* (W. Publishing Group, 1972).

John Wooden and Steve Jamison, *Wooden* (Chicago: McGraw-Hill/ Contemporary Books, 1997).

Index

To Order Additional Copies Of

IF I KNEW THEN
WHAT I KNOW NOW

*Life Skills Strategies for Success
from Today's Student-Athlete Leaders*

Telephone orders: (520) 621-5339 (day); (520) 743-7537 (evening)
Fax Orders: (520) 621-5337
E-mail orders: bell@u.arizona.edu
Website: www.u.arizona.edu/~bell
Postal Orders/Checks payable to:
The Game of Life
3675 W. Dawnbreaker Pl.
Tucson, Arizona 85745

$19.95 per book. Major credit cards accepted.
Shipping: $5.00 for the first item, $1.00 for each additional item

AZ tax: Please add 5.6% sales tax for orders shipped to Arizona
addresses.

Call for information on volume discounts to groups and
associations. Satisfaction guaranteed or your money back!

IF I KNEW THEN WHAT I KNOW NOW
Order Form

Name:..

Address:..

City, State, Zip...

Phone including area code:...

E-Mail:..

Credit Card: ....

Expiration Date:..

# of books............ shipping $............. tax $ .... = total $ ....